Old
Wicked
Songs

To all the great teachers in my life,
especially my parents

OLD
WICKED
SONGS

by
Jon Marans

FIRESIDE THEATRE
GARDEN CITY, NEW YORK

Old Wicked Songs © 1990, 1996 by Jon Marans

ALL RIGHTS RESERVED

SPECIAL NOTE

Originally produced in New York City by
The Barrow Group and Daryl Roth

ISBN 1-56865-273-9
Printed in the United States of America

About the Author

Jon Marans' play, *Old Wicked Songs*, was a 1996 Pulitzer Prize Finalist for Drama and nominated for Best Play by the Drama League. *Old Wicked Songs* was first presented by the Walnut Street Theatre in Philadelphia; then in New York by the Barrow Group and Daryl Roth at Playhouse 91, subsequently moving to the Promenade Theater. It was also produced in England—first at the Bristol Old Vic, then in London's West End at the Gielgud Theater, starring Bob Hoskins.

His play *Child, Child* won the Preston Jones New Play Award in Houston at the Chocolate Bayou Theatre. Mr. Marans' film and television work includes writing for "The New Carol Burnett Show" on CBS and as a script editor for Stonebridge, Michael Douglas' production company at Columbia Pictures.

A graduate of Duke University, Mr. Marans also studied at Lehman Engel's BMI Musical Theatre Workshop and has written lyrics for many composers including Charles Strouse, Edward Thomas, Dan Levine and Galt MacDermot.

OLD WICKED SONGS was produced by Daryl Roth and Jeffrey Ash in association with The Barrow Group at the Promenade Theatre in New York City on August 16, 1996. The associate producers were Frank Basile, Darci Carlton, Elsa Haft and Val Sherman. The general manager was Roy Gabay. It was directed by Seth Barrish; the set and costume designs were by Markas Henry; the lighting design was by Howard Werner; the sound design was by Red Ramona; the vocal consultant was Bill Schuman; casting was by Pat McCorkle and the production stage manager was D. C. Rosenberg. The cast was as follows:

PROFESSOR JOSEF MASHKAN . . . . . Hal Robinson
STEPHEN HOFFMAN . . . . Justin Kirk

OLD WICKED SONGS was originally produced in New York City by The Barrow Group and Daryl Roth Productions, at Playhouse 91/The Jewish Repertory Theatre on October 28, 1995. It was directed by Seth Barrish; the set and costume designs were by Markas Henry; the lighting design was by Howard Werner; the sound design was by One Dream Sound; casting was by Marcia DeBonis; and the production stage manager was D. C. Rosenberg. The cast was as follows:

PROFESSOR JOSEF MASHKAN . . . . Hal Robinson
STEPHEN HOFFMAN . . . . Michael Stuhlbarg

OLD WICKED SONGS received its premiere at the Walnut Street Theatre (Bernard Havard, Executive Director) in Philadelphia, Pennsylvania, on April 25, 1995. It was directed by Frank Ferrante; the set design was by Thom Burnblauskas; the costume design was by Lani Apperson; the lighting design was by Troy Martin-O'Shia; the musical direction was by Jon Marans; the sound design was by Phil Cassidy; and the stage manager was Beth Petitjean. The cast was as follows:

PROFESSOR JOSEF MASHKAN . . . . Hal Robinson
STEPHEN HOFFMAN . . . . Roy Abramsohn

Author's Note

While this is a play, not a musical, almost one third of the show has music in it. Therefore it's vital that every production have a musical director.

In Philadelphia, both actors played the piano. In New York, only Professor Josef Mashkan played, but through the magic of Yamaha, the character of Stephen Hoffman was able to play as well.

For information about the use of Yamaha Disklavier piano, contact: Yamaha Concert and Artists Services, 111 Eighth Avenue, Suite 1531, New York, N.Y. 10019. (212) 366-5753.

The specific pieces used in Act One, Scene 3 for Stephen Hoffman's Disklavier virtuoso playing in New York were:

For the Horowitz hat: *"XI Rhapsodic hongroise,"* Liszt
For the Alfred Brendel hat: "Sonata, Op. 53," Beethoven
For Glenn Gould: "Goldberg Variations, Aria," Bach

"A man's stature is shown by what he mourns and in the way he mourns it."

Bertolt Brecht

Characters

PROFESSOR JOSEF MASHKAN, Viennese, late-50s

STEPHEN HOFFMAN, American, 25 years old

The Scene

OLD WICKED SONGS takes place in Professor Mashkan's rehearsal studio in Vienna, Austria. The play begins in spring of 1986 and continues through to summer.

ACT ONE

Scene 1: Spring afternoon, 1986
Scene 2: Tuesday morning, the next week
Scene 3: Late Wednesday night, two weeks later
Scene 4: Friday afternoon, two days later

ACT TWO

Scene 1: Tuesday morning, two weeks later
Scene 2: Friday afternoon, three days later
Scene 3: Hours later. Night
Scene 4: Tuesday morning, June 10, 1986

CODA: A summer morning.

Old
Wicked
Songs

ACT
I

ACT I

Scene One

TIME: *Spring afternoon, 1986. Vienna, Austria.*

SETTING: *Professor Mashkan's studio. The room is old world Vienna: high ceilings, detailed molding, pre-World War I furniture, worn but comfortable, including an old baby grand piano, a "Habsburg yellow" couch, a coffee table with an empty platter, an empty cup of coffee, a music stand, a gramophone.*

The walls are covered with posters of Klimt, Kokoschka, Makart, and Hampel. The paintings reflect the glitter of early 20th century Vienna, rather than its darker side.

The most prominent item, besides the piano, is a rococo clock. The clock is perpetually set at 5:35.

There are a few cracks on the wall, but they seem to add character rather than make the room look shabby.

A short hallway, stage right, leads to an offstage kitchenette.

Possibly there's a window allowing us to see the city of Vienna. Or better yet, above the confines of the room, the city of Vienna looms.

AT RISE: *Darkness. Then as Mashkan's piano playing is heard, the lights slowly come up, momentarily giving us the feeling we're in a musty cave that's been sealed shut for years.*

As the lights come up to full, bringing us into reality, we see Josef Mashkan, a sly, jolly, mercurial Viennese man in his late 50s, nattily attired—including a colorful vest and bow tie—sitting at his piano, diligently practicing the opening song of Schumann's song cycle: "Dichterliebe." He makes an error, stops and then plays the passage again, still hitting the same wrong note. Mashkan slaps the finger that played the wrong note.

MASHKAN (*playfully angry*): Nein. Nein nein nein nein nein!

(*Mashkan begins playing the piece again.*)

There's a knocking at the door, but Mashkan is too deep in thought to hear it as he softly sings along to "Im wunderschönen Monat Mai")

MASHKAN (*sings*):
IM WUNDERSCHÖNEN MONAT MAI
ALS ALLE KNOSPEN SPRANGEN
DA IST IN MEINEM HERZEN
DIE LIEBE AUFGEGANGEN

(*Meanwhile, a young man, Stephen Hoffman, has opened the door and peered in, watching Mashkan play. Stephen Hoffman is a 25 year old prodigy. He's a somewhat arrogant, socially awkward, high-energy, light-haired man dressed conservatively in a jacket, tie, and pressed pants*)

STEPHEN (*interrupting music, showing off*): Schumann. Opus 48. You're playing it in C sharp minor. It was originally written in F sharp minor.

MASHKAN (*in German*): Sind Sie ohne Klopfen herein-
gekommen! [You entered without knocking!]

STEPHEN: I knocked. No one answered.

MASHKAN (*in German*): Und sie kommen einfach herein?
[So you walk right in?]

STEPHEN: The door was unlocked. Isn't this part of the
university?

MASHKAN (*in German*): Ich arbeite an der Universität. Das
ist mein Atelier! [*I* am part of the university. *This* is my
studio!]

STEPHEN: Is this 315?

MASHKAN (*in English*): Give me your name.

STEPHEN: Hey, I didn't mean to disturb you—

MASHKAN: I am asking for your name—to report you for
lack of manners.

STEPHEN (*getting defensive*): What is this? High school?
. . . Stephen. Stephen Hoffman. And now, if you could
tell me where 315 is?

MASHKAN (*suddenly nervous*): But today is Wednesday.

STEPHEN: Yeah?

MASHKAN: Stephen Hoffman is not arriving until Friday.
Today is Wednesday!

STEPHEN: I took an earlier flight.

(*Pause*)

MASHKAN (*suddenly enthusiastic*): Well, come in my boy. This is 315. Come in. I don't know why I snapped at you. Please accept my apology. Uncalled for. Completely uncalled for. Maybe we should start new because I feel bad about what just occurred and I really do apolo—well, I can't say that again, can I? . . . So Grüss Gott.

(*Beat*)

STEPHEN: Are you talking to me?

MASHKAN: Entschuldigung. I mean . . . excuse me. I thought you knew German.

STEPHEN: Ein wenig. [Translation: A little]

MASHKAN: Ein wenig and you do not understand "Grüss Gott"?

STEPHEN: Nein.

MASHKAN: Ah, curious. . . . I think I need some more coffee. I'll get you some, too.

STEPHEN: No, I'm giving it up.

MASHKAN: Nonsense.

STEPHEN: Really. It makes me way too tense.

MASHKAN: How much tenser can you get?! A cup will not kill you.
(*Mashkan exits to kitchenette to get coffee. Stephen sits down*)
And please, take your seat.
(*Poking his head back in, not pleased*)
Ah, you have taken . . . Fine.

(*Mashkan reexits*)

STEPHEN (*surveying the room—doesn't like it*): Old place you've got here.

MASHKAN (*offstage*): Thank you.

STEPHEN (*surprised*): You like it?

MASHKAN (*offstage*): Ja. Doesn't everyone?

STEPHEN (*arrogant without realizing it*): I guess I've been spoiled by modern architecture. You know, simple beauty. Clean lines. Nothing gaudy. I grew up in California.

MASHKAN (*offstage*): How lucky for you.

STEPHEN (*seeing newspapers on coffee table*): So Kurt Waldheim's making headlines in Austria, too?

MASHKAN (*offstage*): Well, ja, we *are* the ones electing him president.

STEPHEN (*embarrassed*): Oh, right. . . . You really think he's a Nazi?

MASHKAN (*offstage, momentarily taken aback by his direct-ness*): . . . It's 1986. Who cares? . . . What do *you* think?

STEPHEN (*standing up, going to the piano*): What do I know? I'm a musician.
(*To himself*)
Or was.

(*Stephen circles the piano as if he were about to wrestle it.*

He lightly kicks a leg, then jokingly jumps away as if it would kick him back.

Meanwhile, Mashkan has reentered, carrying a small silver tray with coffee. He silently watches on as Stephen takes three deep breaths & tugs his ears three times; and then lunges at the piano as if he were diving into a pool. Stephen immediately plays the opening bars of "Im wunderschönen Monat Mai," playing swiftly and technically perfect, but without emotion.

Suddenly he stops playing in mid-measure)

STEPHEN (*to himself*): Now who the hell is *this?!*

(*Stephen smacks his hand* hard *against his head. So hard that we feel he actually hurt it.*

Silence. Mashkan, uneasy at what he has just seen, backs out of the room and then says before reentering)

MASHKAN: I'm bringing out the coffee.

ACT I

(*Mashkan enters*)

STEPHEN: Oh good. I could use some after all.

MASHKAN (*uneasy*): But if it makes you tense, maybe you shouldn't have any.

STEPHEN (*firmly*): No I want it.

MASHKAN: Fine.
(*Stephen drinks the coffee down in one shot and begins pouring more. Nervous*)
So, when did you arrive in Wien? In Vienna?

STEPHEN: Last night.

MASHKAN: You've been here a night and a morning and no one said "Grüss Gott"?

STEPHEN: I haven't spoken to anyone.

MASHKAN: Ja, but to ask directions?

STEPHEN: I find things by myself.

MASHKAN: How very independent. . . . Well when Austrians greet each other, they always say Grüss Gott. It means "may god greet you." So, Grüss Gott, Stephen Hoffman.

STEPHEN: Grüss Gott, Professor Schiller.

MASHKAN: Oh, nein. Professor Mashkan.

STEPHEN: . . . What?

MASHKAN: To study piano accompaniment with Herr Schiller, you must first study singing with me for three months. To understand how the singer feels. These are Professor Schiller's instructions. He must have told you.

STEPHEN (*quiet intensity*): He said something about me learning to be respectful of singers, but I was certain I'd talked him out of it. When he told me to report to Room 315, I assumed it was his studio.
(*Said slowly as if Mashkan were stupid*)
I'm not a singer. I play the piano.

MASHKAN: What's the fuss? It is hardly unusual for an accompanist to study singing.

STEPHEN: Maybe in college. I'm 25.

MASHKAN: Ancient.

STEPHEN: What's Professor Schiller's number?

MASHKAN: He is away for a few weeks to Munich. A music conference. But I will give you his secretary's number if you want.

STEPHEN: Please.

MASHKAN (*as he writes it down, amused*): *Schiller* will not change his mind. When a Jew makes a deal, he sticks to it. Remember "The Merchant of Venice"!

(*He hands Stephen the number. Stephen is silent, uneasy at the remark*)
So, let us review your schedule.

STEPHEN: It's a little stuffy in here, don't you think?

MASHKAN: I will open a window.

(*He heads over*)

STEPHEN: Schiller's in Munich?

MASHKAN: Ja.

STEPHEN: How far is that from here?

MASHKAN: Five hours by train. . . . You're not thinking of going there now?

STEPHEN (*uneasy*): No. I just—uh—promised someone I'd go there eventually.

MASHKAN: You are very secretive. . . . I like that.

STEPHEN: You know, this isn't going to work. I should get going.

(*Stephen heads toward the door*)

MASHKAN: I'll bet you're lousy in bed.

(*Stephen stops*)

STEPHEN: What?

MASHKAN: You are, aren't you?

STEPHEN: What's that got to do with—I mean, not that I am! But what's that got to—

MASHKAN (*moving closer to Stephen*): Have you ever really had good sex?

STEPHEN (*thinking Mashkan's coming on to him*): I like them younger. And with breasts.

MASHKAN: So do I! . . . I only say you are lousy in bed because I believe there is a direct correlation between making love to a woman and making love to a piano. And judging by the way you just made love to a piano—

STEPHEN: You saw me?! That's not fair. You should've told me right away you were in the room!

MASHKAN: Ah, the way you did when I was playing? It is lucky I was here. You almost tried to rape my piano! She must be flirted with, not pounced on. Caress her keys. Let her know she is safe in your arms. Once that is established, *then* you can be wild and passionate. Come. Stand here. Let me show you how a seduction is done. First admire her smooth, shiny skin.
(*Running his hands along the piano's keys*)
See her warm, bright smile.

STEPHEN: Half of her teeth are blacked out.

MASHKAN (*amused*): That was funny. I knew you had it in you—somewhere. Come. Smile back at her.

STEPHEN: This is silly.

MASHKAN: What can you lose?

STEPHEN: My dignity.

MASHKAN: Flirt with her. Run your hand through her strings.
(*Mashkan slowly strums the strings. The sound is almost mystical, other-worldly. We see Mashkan absorbed in the sound*)
Like so, Stefan.

STEPHEN: My name's Stephen.

MASHKAN: In America, Stephen, but here in Wien, "Stefan." "Vienna," "Wien." "Stephen," "Stefan." Ja, Stefan?

STEPHEN (*silent*)

MASHKAN: You're getting tense again. Strum.
(*Stephen quickly strums the strings*)
Slower.

(*Stephen strums—a tad slower*)

STEPHEN (*hurting himself on the strings*): Ow!

MASHKAN: What happened?

STEPHEN: I scraped myself on the strings.

MASHKAN: Perhaps she gave you a love bite! . . . I think it's too soon for touching or flirting. First you must get acquainted. That's the key.

(*He quickly plays a note*)

Get it. The key!

(*Quickly plays note again. Stephen isn't amused*)

Consider the next three months an old-fashioned courtship between you and this very grand Grand. Just communicating through looks and sounds. You singing Schumann's song cycle "Dichterliebe," "The Poet's Love," while *she* accompanies *you.*

(*Mashkan hands Stephen a book from the piano*)

Here. I already bought you the "Dichterliebe." It costs fifty schillings, but I am giving it to you as a gift. Thirty schillings.

(*Mashkan holds out his hand. Stephen is momentarily confused, but then reluctantly pays*)

Study the first song for next Tuesday. We will have lessons Tuesday mornings and Friday afternoons.

STEPHEN: Professor, I'm sure you're a fine musician—

MASHKAN: Mashkan, call me Mashkan. All my university students do.

STEPHEN: Let's face it. This is a waste of your time and mine.

MASHKAN: I disagree. An accompanist must know how a singer feels.

STEPHEN: And what if I don't care how they feel?

MASHKAN (*dead serious*): . . . Then you can never be a good accompanist . . . So, I will see you next Tuesday. Study "Im wunderschönen Monat Mai." Page one. Also, please see the operas "Cavalleria Rusticana" and "Der Bajazzo" this weekend so we can discuss the singers. Opera is an important part of my class. (*Motioning him to the door*) Until Tuesday.

STEPHEN: We'll see.

(*Stephen starts towards door*)

MASHKAN: It would be unwise to skip this class. Professor Schiller would not be happy.
(*Off a look from Stephen*)
Please, I know why you're here. You are not just an accompanist. You are a very fine soloist. A prodigy. Or should I say were—since you have not performed for almost a year. After so many concerts at such an early age, you burn out. And now you are scared the flame will not go on again. Understandable. Of all the American professors you have gone to, none have rekindled your joy for music. In desperation, you fly all the way to Vienna to study with the famous Professor Schiller. And what does he tell you? You will not study solo pieces— but rather be an accompanist for voice. Very humbling. And further, before you study accompaniment, you must study singing. More humbling. I suppose it might make one feel nervous about one's talent. Make one wonder if he should have been a pianist at all. A scary thought for someone who has dedicated his life to music. Very very scary. I suppose it might even make one a little defensive, a little—arrogant . . . Auf Wiedersehen, Stefan. Until Tuesday.

15

STEPHEN (*still defensive*): You don't say Grüss Gott when you leave? It's not like shalom or aloha?!

MASHKAN: Auf Wiedersehen.
(*Stephen starts to leave*)
Oh, wait! I made a key for you. I only use this studio during the day. Since your dormitory is out past the Ringstrasse, you might go to the opera one night and miss the last train—they stop at midnight. Please feel free to stay here.
(*Stephen takes the key and exits*)
You are welcome.

(*For a moment Mashkan sits, his enthusiasm and energy gone. Then he accepts the challenge of this new student, chuckles, swiftly takes a pill, swallowing it down with his coffee and goes to the piano with renewed determination.*)

Mashkan begins practicing "Im wunderschönen Monat Mai" again. He makes another mistake, winces at it, then continues playing. As the lights fade down on him, we should once again feel as if we're back in that musty cave mentioned in the opening. As the lights fade to black, they wrap Mashkan in darkness)

End of Scene One

MUSICAL NOTE
At the end of the scene, as Mashkan plays the first song of the "Dichterliebe," a recorded version comes in, perfectly aligned to Mashkan's playing. The recorded version grows louder and louder, eventually taking over Mashkan's piano playing, gloriously filling the theater.

In darkness, we hear about half of the first song—until it's interrupted by a musical chord played by Mashkan which leads us into Scene Two.

AUTHOR'S NOTE
At the end of scene one and at the end of every scene throughout the play, different songs from the "Dichterliebe" are heard. These very specific song choices serve two vital purposes. They are integral to the drama of the play, heightening the lead-out of scenes and emotionally aiding the lead-ins to the next scene. Also, they allow the audience the chance to hear these songs in order, thus helping them more deeply absorb the emotional impact of Schumann's song cycle. Therefore, the songs listed should not be altered. Consider them as much a part of the text as the dialogue.

ACT I

Scene Two

SETTING: *Mashkan's studio. Tuesday morning. The next week.*

AT RISE: *Mashkan plays a chord which stops the recorded music. At the same time, the lights crash up and we see Mashkan at the piano and Stephen standing. Mashkan starts on middle C and plays a five note scale up and down, singing AH to each note.*

MASHKAN: Your turn.

(Stephen sings the 9 AHs as Mashkan plays the notes. Stephen is not too terrible)

STEPHEN: I called Professor Schiller's secretary—
(Mashkan interrupts Stephen by repeating the chord and then modulating up a half. [Throughout this section, as Stephen sings his AHs, Mashkan tries to keep Stephen in strict rhythm.] Stephen, a little annoyed, jumps in and sings the five note scale as Mashkan plays the piano)
     AH AH AH AH AH AH AH AH AH—
(Jumping in, speaking)
     —she gave me his number in Munich. He told me—
(Mashkan interrupts by playing chord and then modulating up a half step. Stephen, more annoyed, sings)
     AH AH AH AH AH AH AH AH AH—
(Speaking)
     —to hold out for three weeks. And then decide. So I
     made—
(Mashkan plays chord and then half-step modulation. Stephen continues talking—very quickly)

18

an appointment three weeks from this Friday and then this nightmare will be over!
(*Singing, triumphantly*)
AH AH AH AH AH AH AH AH AH!

MASHKAN: Thank you for the information.

(*Mashkan plays chord and half-step modulation*)

STEPHEN (*interrupting*): —also, I want you to know right upfront—at this first lesson—that as long as I'm here I won't be happy!
(*Singing*)
AH AH AH AH AH AH AH AH AH!

MASHKAN: Well that will make teaching you so much fun.

(*Mashkan plays chord and half-step modulation*)

STEPHEN: Sigmund Freud, one of Vienna's own, would applaud me. I'm expressing myself!

MASHKAN: Ah!

STEPHEN (*singing, exuberantly*):
AH AH AH AH AH AH AH AH AH!

MASHKAN: Sometimes I wonder why Freud insisted people be so forthright. After all, if we can do nothing about a situation, why complain? Most of us cannot enjoy everything we do in life and yet we throw off the blankets and get out of the bed each morning.

STEPHEN: The covers.

MASHKAN: What?

STEPHEN: Throw off the covers.

MASHKAN: Ah, the covers. Thank you for the English lesson.

(*Mashkan continues playing higher up the scale. Stephen's voice cracks*)

STEPHEN: You'd better not be laughing.

MASHKAN: There was nothing to laugh at . . . You are slouching.

STEPHEN: The stand is too low.

MASHKAN: There was no music to read. Stop making excuses. Stand straight. It will help the sound come out. (*Stephen stands straight as Mashkan gets up and starts removing Stephen's jacket. Stephen is uncomfortable being touched*)
You need to be comfortable singing.

(*Mashkan starts to remove the tie*)

STEPHEN (*stopping Mashkan*): I always wear a tie.

MASHKAN: It's strangling you.

STEPHEN: It reminds me I'm alive.

MASHKAN: I think there are easier ways. . . . You are stranger than you look. . . . I like that. Breathe for me.

(*Stephen breathes. Mashkan puts his hand on Stephen's lower stomach. Stephen jumps back*)

I have an adoring wife and get no joy touching you. Of course, after so many years I get no joy touching my wife!

(*Mashkan laughs wildly. Stephen is silent*)

It's a joke. Stand next to me. It's the only way I can tell what you're doing.

(*Stephen moves next to Mashkan who puts his hand back on Stephen's stomach*)

In. . . . Out. . . . In . . . out. . . . You're breathing wrong.

STEPHEN: It's kept me going all these years.

MASHKAN: You must breathe from the diaphragm. This will give you greater breath control. Try it. In . . . out . . . in . . . out. No, no, no. Touch my stomach.

(*Stephen hesitates and then touches Mashkan's upper stomach*)

Lower.

(*Stephen moves his hand slightly lower*)

Lower.

(*Stephen barely moves it. Mashkan moves Stephen's hand lower and then breathes*)

Feel the difference when I breathe. It comes not from the throat but deep within. In. Out. In. Out.

(*Mashkan stops. Stephen, fascinated, doesn't realize he's finished*)

You may remove your hand unless you are enjoying it.

(*Stephen quickly moves his hand away. Mashkan chuckles*)

Work on that at home. Also, you must learn to open your throat more. Say "Ah."

STEPHEN (*almost closed mouthed*): Ah.

MASHKAN (*with a widely opened mouth*): AHH!

STEPHEN (*still not opening his mouth much*): Ah.

(*Beat*)

MASHKAN: As I said, work on that at home. . . . Let's start at the beginning of "Im wunderschönen."

(*Mashkan plays the piano cautiously at first, starting out slowly, then surging and speeding up at rising sequences, then pulling back the last three notes of each phrase before surging ahead again into the next phrase. Stephen conducts to himself, but finds it difficult since Mashkan keeps changing the beat*)

STEPHEN (*sings, jumping in a little too early because of Mashkan's erratic playing*):
IM WUNDERSCHÖNEN MONAT MAI
ALS ALLE KNOSPEN SPRANGEN
(*Mashkan speeds up. Stephen must jump in again*)
DA IST IN MEINEM HERZEN
DIE LIEBE AUFGEGAGEN

(*Mashkan stops*)

MASHKAN: You have a pleasant voice. Certainly not great— or even good. But pleasant.

STEPHEN: Thanks for the pat on the back.

MASHKAN: But you have a counting problem. You came in early at "die liebe" and "Im wunderschönen."

STEPHEN: The accompanist changed tempos!

MASHKAN: I see you find it easier to blame others than to accept your own failings.

STEPHEN: I may not sing well, but I have a perfect inner clock.
(*Pointing to music*)
This says adagio. Adagio has not existed today.

MASHKAN: It has for me.

STEPHEN: Where's a metronome?

MASHKAN: I don't need one.

STEPHEN (*spotting the clock, heading towards it*): I'll figure it out by the clock.

MASHKAN: That may be a little difficult since it has not moved for over 10 years. The weights—they're unbalanced.

STEPHEN: Clock imitating life?

MASHKAN (*amused*): I should not laugh since it was directed at me—but it is so rare you make a joke. . . . Now please, return to your stand.

(*Stephen does. Mashkan begins to play. He starts slowly and then picks up the pace*)

STEPHEN: Speeding up.

MASHKAN: It's my solo. I have dramatic license.

STEPHEN: An accompanist is there solely for the singer. Begin again.

MASHKAN: I will not. You missed your cue.

STEPHEN (*briskly*): Not by my count.

MASHKAN (*annoyed, stops playing*): . . . I am not solely a metronome for a singer. I must immerse myself into the song. And if that calls for speeding up a little or slowing down during piano solos, ist gut. Art consists of knowing the basic rules and realizing when it is time to deviate from them. You don't want to be just a robot—always sticking to the precise rules, do you Stefan?

STEPHEN (*tightly*): Stephen.

(*Beat*)

MASHKAN (*lightly*): Again. From the top.

(*Mashkan begins playing again*)

STEPHEN (*sings, mispronouncing "wun"*): IM WUNDER—

MASHKAN (*a rounder sound*): Wun.

STEPHEN (*incorrectly*): Wun.

MASHKAN: Lighter. Rounder. Wun.

STEPHEN (*correctly, though getting annoyed*): Wun.

MASHKAN: Again.

STEPHEN (*correctly*): Wunwunwunwunwun!

MASHKAN (*congratulating Stephen*): Wunderbar!

(*Mashkan gives Stephen his pitch*)

STEPHEN (*sings*):
   IM WUN—

MASHKAN: Gut!

STEPHEN (*Sings*):
   —DERSCHÖNEN MONAT MAI
   ALS ALLE KNOSPEN—
(*Spoken*)
   You're speeding up!
(*Sings, catching up*)
   . . . SPRANGEN
(*Spoken*)
   Slowing down!
(*Sings*)
   DA IST IN MEINEM HERZEN
(*Mashkan hits a wrong note, spoken*)
   D natural!

(*Mashkan stops*)

MASHKAN (*hurt*): I am a vocal coach, not an accompanist. I haven't practiced this for many months. You do not need to yell at me! . . . Let us go over the words, for meaning.

STEPHEN: I understand them.

MASHKAN: Poetry is difficult. Especially German. It's a little more subtle than covers and blankets. Let me hear your translation.

STEPHEN (*without emotion*): In the wonderful month of May, when all the trees were blooming—

MASHKAN: Stop.

STEPHEN: Those are the words.

MASHKAN: But not the feelings. (*With heartfelt emotion*) "Im wunderschönen Monat Mai." In the loveliest of months—May.

STEPHEN (*without emotion*): Right. In the wonderful month of May.

MASHKAN (*with spirit*): "Als alle knospen sprangen."

STEPHEN (*without emotion*): When all the trees were blooming.

MASHKAN: Not just blooming—sprangen—bursting in bloom! You know, like sex. It's spring.

"Da ist in meinem herzen, die liebe aufgegangen." Go ahead.

STEPHEN (*still without emotion*): I felt in my heart, love assuming.

MASHKAN: Love *assuming?* . . . No no no. Love opened up in *my* heart as well. Listen to the whole thing.

In the loveliest of months—May,
when the buds are bursting in bloom,
love opened up in *my* heart as well.

This is manly love *and* feminine love. Manly in its strength. Feminine, its beauty—like Vienna itself. Look at our city when you stroll about. See the firm old buildings, the thick solid walls. But notice the flourishes—the statues, the arches, the molding, the cornices, the facades, each different from the next. Each building eventually rising to a peak, but so many choices for the eye to find its way to the top. Not like your modern American box buildings which lead the eye straight up—without any chance to find undiscovered beauty.

STEPHEN: Modern architecture is just a streamlining of your buildings.

MASHKAN: Ah, streamlining. A very evocative sounding word, but what does it mean? Stripping art of all its beauty until it is reduced to science. Just as modern composers streamline music, remove the emotion, reduce music to mathematical theory. Give me too much passion to none at all! . . . Stefan, stop thinking like your simplistic modern American music and architec-

27

ture. Life is not always so clearcut. There is a mind
inside of here. Make it work. . . . Now sing again.
With more passion!

(*Mashkan begins to play*)

STEPHEN (*sings, overly exuberant*):
IM WUNDERSCHÖNEN MONAT MAI—

MASHKAN: Not Broadway! I don't need teeth and eyes. I
need true feelings. Think of one of your girlfriends in
college. The need to just see her, but you know you
must wait for classes to end. And the waiting seems like
an eternity.

STEPHEN: I enjoyed my classes. Besides, my girlfriends
were more—
(*A little embarrassed*)
the intellectual type.

MASHKAN: Why am I not surprised? . . . You *must* feel
passionate about something.

STEPHEN: Dropping this class!

MASHKAN: Good! Then use that. Now passion.

(*Mashkan begins to play*)

STEPHEN: But it doesn't make sense! The words are hokey
and overly romantic while the music is melancholy—

MASHKAN (*interrupting*): That is the whole point—

STEPHEN (*continuing his thought*): —look, it starts and ends on a discord in a minor key!

MASHKAN: This is a song remembering the youthful passion—(*more personal*) which is now gone. Listen to the prelude.

(*Mashkan plays again, very sensitively*)

STEPHEN: Speeding up.
(*Mashkan hits a wrong note*)
    D#.

(*Mashkan stops*)

MASHKAN: You play it! You're the pianist!
(*Stephen circles the piano as he did before and then starts to almost pounce on it. Mashkan points to the piano*)
    Be gentle with her!
(*Stephen sits. He breathes and tugs his ears three times—trying to be as subtle as possible doing it—and then begins playing*)
    Why do you do that?

STEPHEN (*feigning innocence*): Do what?

MASHKAN: Breathe and tug.

STEPHEN: I don't know what you're talking about.

MASHKAN: Stop playing.
(*Stephen keeps playing*)
    Stop playing!

(*Stephen stops*)
Now start again. Without breathing or tugging.

(*Stephen tries but each time his hands go back to his ears*)

That's not fair!

MASHKAN (*feigning innocence as well*): I don't know what you're talking about.

STEPHEN: It's my mother's fault. She's superstitious. She thinks everything good comes in threes. So I breathe and tug three times.

MASHKAN: And what should this accomplish?

STEPHEN: Helping me play right.

MASHKAN: How is right?

STEPHEN: I don't know.

MASHKAN: . . . Begin again.

STEPHEN: And it's okay if I—?

(*Stephen breathes and tugs*)

MASHKAN: Ja, ja.

(*Stephen breathes and tugs again and then plays too quickly*)

Listen carefully to what you're playing.

(*Stephen stops playing*)

> See how the music sounds like someone thinking back, slowly remembering the month of May.

(*Stephen plays again, this time with more sensitivity*)

> As the singer comes in, the tonality lightens, but the first notes still recall the sad opening—
> (*Sings*)
> IM WUNDERSCHÖNEN MONAT MAI
> (*Spoken*)
> Sing along.

(*Stephen softly plays and sings as Mashkan speaks—[when the words are in CAPS, Mashkan also sings]*)

MASHKAN: ALS ALLE KNOSPEN SPRANGEN. Still hesitant and then the love builds. DA IST IN MEINEM HERZEN and builds LIEBE AUF—and *builds!* and then the sad prelude again. Happiness, but only for a moment.

STEPHEN (*softly*): I see.

MASHKAN (*as MUSIC continues*): Now joy is about to begin again, but first the dissonant appogiatura on WUNDERSCHÖNEN. Then another rising sequence as before which lifts ALLE VÖGEL SANGEN and then falls DA HAB' ICH IHR GESTANDEN and then lifts again. He speaks of his loves and his longings.
(*With great longing*)
VERLANGEN. But his longings are not answered. The prelude comes back in again, ending with an unresolved

dominant seventh, reminding us of the sadness throughout.

(*Stephen ends the song noticeably moved. Mashkan's teaching was magical. As Mashkan lets the last note linger in his mind, Stephen interrupts*)

STEPHEN: Let's do it again.

MASHKAN: Not so fast my friend. Savor the moment.

STEPHEN (*controlled excitement*): No, you don't understand. I haven't felt this good playing the piano. . . .

(*Stephen breathes & tugs and starts to play*)

MASHKAN: What are you doing?

STEPHEN: Recreating the moment.

MASHKAN: I am glad you are happy with my teaching, but please wait.
(*Stephen continues playing, lost in the music*)
I told you to stop playing. You must savor the experience.
(*Stephen still continues playing*)
Stefan! I am closing the piano. I will slam this down on your hands if you do not stop!

(*Stephen, desperately trying to recreate the feeling, ignores Mashkan. Mashkan slams the piano lid down. Stephen removes his hands in the nick of time*)

STEPHEN (*furious*): You could've ended my career!

MASHKAN: I am the teacher, not you. *You* listen to *me!*

STEPHEN: I didn't want to lose it!

MASHKAN: You cannot lose what you do not yet understand! Take a deep breath! Now!

STEPHEN (*angry*): I was giving you a compliment!—

MASHKAN: A deep breath!
(*Stephen does, half-heartedly*)
Now close your eyes . . . Close them.
(*Stephen does, warily*)
Allow the song to swim about in your brain. Think back. Absorb the feeling of
(*Sung*)
IM WUNDERSCHÖNEN MONAT MAI
(*Spoken*)
Words filled with joy accompanied by wistful, melancholy sounds.
(*Singing*)
ALS ALLE KNOSPEN SPRANGEN
Can you hear it? . . . Can you?
(*Stephen nods*)
This combination of joy and sadness—this is the core of truly beautiful music. Just as it is the core of drama. Of life. For instance, when you left for Vienna what did your mother say to you?

STEPHEN (*like a bratty kid*): Let Stephen play the song once more!

MASHKAN: That is not what she said.

STEPHEN: She said "for once, Stephen, go and enjoy yourself." And then she hugged me. And cried.

MASHKAN: She was obviously sad you were leaving—yet still happy you would have this experience. Sadness and joy. When a composer finds both, the result is Mozart. Beethoven. And how do they acquire this perfect combination? Why do some countries give us great composers, while others not? Take England. Good composers, like Benjamin Britten, but no musical geniuses. And few great singers. Why? Because England has not had prolonged national suffering. Since the days of the Romans, they have not been invaded. And having never lived through great sadness, they have little comprehension of great joy. However, here in Austria and in Germany, our soil has been ravaged by two world wars. Before that, invaded many times. And we have Schubert, Brahms, Schumann. And great singers like Leonie Rysaneck . . . Curiously, Japan has few great composers or singers.

STEPHEN: Because Japan hasn't been invaded?

MASHKAN: . . . It's a theory.

STEPHEN: Wait a minute! Two atomic bombs were dropped on Japan.

MASHKAN: A catastrophe. No denying. But there is a big difference between two cities annihilated in seconds and a country bearing centuries of oppression—as Korea felt under Japan's rule! I would place my bets there is great undiscovered musical talent in Korea.

STEPHEN: So the United States can't have great artists since we've never been invaded?

MASHKAN: No. Leontyne Price is great. Of course she is black and black people have definitely been oppressed.

STEPHEN: Okay, I see.
(*Enjoying the game*)
   Then Jessye Norman is great.

MASHKAN: Possibly.

STEPHEN: And on the piano, Vladimir Horowitz!

MASHKAN: Since when is he black?

STEPHEN: He's Jewish. The Jews have certainly suffered.

MASHKAN: I don't think so.

STEPHEN: The Jews haven't suffered?

MASHKAN: I don't think Horowitz is great. Too schmaltzy.

STEPHEN: Then Leonard Bernstein. As a conductor.

MASHKAN: The man jumps up and down onstage.

STEPHEN: They go wild for him here.

MASHKAN: I enjoy him also. But not great.

STEPHEN: All right. Mahler! Viennese *and* Jewish. How much worse could one person suffer?

MASHKAN: You're not Jewish . . . are you?

STEPHEN: No. Protestant.

MASHKAN: Ah yes, one of those lapsed Catholics. I didn't think you were Jewish. You certainly don't look it. Have a pastry.
(*Stephen takes one and bites into it*)
Delicious, ja? And only twenty schillings, please.
(*Stephen laughs*)
What's so funny?

STEPHEN: Your joke.

MASHKAN: What joke was that?

STEPHEN: . . . nothing.

(*Stephen pays*)

MASHKAN (*changing the subject*): So how did you like the operas this weekend?

STEPHEN (*still uneasy over Mashkan's comments about Jews*): They were fine.

MASHKAN: You've seen "Cavalleria Rusticana" and "Der Bajazzo" before?

STEPHEN: No, but I've heard them.

MASHKAN: And the difference?

STEPHEN: Some snoring businessmen sitting in front of me.

MASHKAN (*lightly laughing*): Some snoring businessmen— (*Suddenly angry*)
I shouldn't have let you eat my pastry!

STEPHEN: What?

MASHKAN: I did not want you to have one anyway!

STEPHEN (*confused*): You asked if I wanted any. And charged me for it!

MASHKAN: In Vienna, if you offer something just once, the other person is supposed to say "no"! Only if the giver persists two more times do you really know he wants you to have it! If I could, I would rip that pastry from you but you've already stuffed half of it down your throat! All Americans devour food. You take no time to appreciate anything!

STEPHEN: I'll eat slower. Jesus.

MASHKAN: And do not take his name in vain!

STEPHEN: Why are you so angry?

MASHKAN: You have disappointed me!

STEPHEN: I said I'd eat slower!

MASHKAN: I'm not talking about the pastry! . . . At least when I first met you, I thought you were honest! Maybe obnoxious and opinionated, but honest.

STEPHEN: I am!

MASHKAN: The first time going to the Staatsoper, seeing that hall, hearing that music, it is always a thrill! You did not go, did you?

STEPHEN: I was planning on going—

MASHKAN: No you weren't! You didn't go just to spite me. Is that not so?!

STEPHEN (*suddenly, with great anger*): That's right, it is! And maybe I'll do it again! Just remember, *I don't need this class!*

(*Pause*)

MASHKAN (*puzzled*): Why are you so upset? I'm the one who's supposed to be angry at you.

(*Stephen is silent. Mashkan goes to the piano*)

Let us start again. "Im wunderschönen Monat Mai."

STEPHEN: Just like that?

MASHKAN: What do you want? More scolding? This is not high school.
(*Looking at schedule on table*)
There's another performance of operas two weeks from this Wednesday—if you decide to go.

(*As Mashkan starts to play, Stephen interrupts him*)

STEPHEN: Mashkan.

MASHKAN: Ja?

STEPHEN: You're playing the piano.

MASHKAN (*checking to see, tongue-in-cheek*): So I am.

STEPHEN: I would really like to play.

MASHKAN: You are the singer. I play the piano.

(*Mashkan plays. He hits a wrong note. Stephen winces*)

STEPHEN: That's debatable.

(*Mashkan continues playing "Im wunderschönen" as lights fade to black*)

End Scene Two

MUSICAL NOTE
Again, the recorded music picks up what Mashkan plays and then segues into the second song of the "Dichterliebe" ("Aus meinen Tranen spriessen").

LIGHTING NOTE
Half-way through the second song, lights slowly come up and we find ourselves in a sort of operatic, darkly-lit, half-in-shadows, nether world. We see Mashkan, a little tipsy, lighting a cigarette. As he smokes, it's almost as if he hears the second song of the cycle in his head—for as the song ends, he allows the silence to ring out for a moment, just as it would if it were actually being played in the cycle. Then he proceeds to play the third song—half in darkness—as we find ourselves in . . .

ACT I

Scene Three

SETTING: *Mashkan's studio. Late Wednesday night, two weeks later. Only the piano light is on. There is a box of pastries on the table and a glass of whiskey on the side of the piano.*

AT RISE: *Mashkan is at the piano, singing and playing "Die Rose, die Lilie, die Taube" (the third song in the "Dichterliebe"). The song is played "Munter"—at a bright clip. Mashkan's speech is slightly slurred. He's quite jolly.*

MASHKAN:
"DIE ROSE, DIE LILIE, DIE TAUBE, DIE
    SONNE
DIE LIEBT' ICH EINST ALLE IN
    LIEBESWONNE
ICH LIEB' SIE NICHT MEHR,
ICH LIEBE ALLEINE DIE KLEINE, DIE
    FEINE, DIE REINE, DIE EINE;
SIE SELBER ALLER LIEBE WONNE,
IST ROSE UND LILIE UND TAUBE UND
    SONNE,
ICH LIEBE ALLEINE DIE KLEINE,
DIE FEINE, DIE REINE, DIE EINE, DIE EINE!

(Toasting himself, pleased with his performance)

Nicht so schlimm. [Not so bad.]

(A key is heard unlocking the door. Mashkan stops playing.

*Stephen hurls open the door and, thinking he's alone, be-
gins exuberantly singing the aria "Vesti la Giubba" from "I
Pagliacci." He wears a large, green hat)*

STEPHEN (*sings*):
   AH! RIDI PAGLIACCIO
   SULTUO AMORE INFRANTO!
   ["Laugh clown over your shattered love"]

(*In the middle of Stephen's singing, Mashkan continues the
aria, exuberantly playing and singing—very much startling
Stephen*)

MASHKAN:
   RIDI DEL DUOL
   CHE T'AVELENA IL COR!

(*Mashkan then laughs—as the clown would laugh*)

STEPHEN (*embarrassed*): Entschuldigung. I didn't know
   you'd still be here. . . . Sorry 'bout the singing. I'm
   out of here.

MASHKAN: No, stay. I am leaving soon.
(*Seeing Stephen's hat*)
   Nice hat.

STEPHEN: I bought it tonight. It's Tyrolean. That means
   from Tyrol.

MASHKAN: Really?

STEPHEN (*embarrassed*): I guess you knew that.

MASHKAN: Very spiffy. But you're wearing it wrong.

(*Mashkan pulls it all the way down over Stephen's face*)

STEPHEN: Even you can't get to me tonight. I'm too up.

MASHKAN (*pulling hat back up and knocking it off*): Then forget it.

STEPHEN: You're working late.

MASHKAN: I have been told I need to practice—if I hope to keep a student.

STEPHEN: Your piano playing has nothing to do with—
(*Suddenly stopping that thought*)
. . . Your wife must be worried you're not home yet.

MASHKAN: Since she's been dead over ten years, I doubt it.

STEPHEN (*embarrassed*): I thought . . . just a couple of weeks ago you said you were married—

MASHKAN (*said very tongue-in-cheek*): I say that so I will not look so lonely and pitiful. Do you think it worked?!

(*Beat*)

STEPHEN: Are you all right?

MASHKAN: Tremendous!

(*Mashkan hits a C major chord*)

STEPHEN (*feeling uneasy*): I should get home.

MASHKAN: The U-Bahn stopped running at midnight.

STEPHEN: I'll get a cab—

MASHKAN (*suddenly angry*): I said I am leaving! Stay!
(*Jolly again*)
> That was some smile on your face when you came in.
> You either just had a woman or went to the operas. Or
> both.
(*Seeing Stephen eyeing the pastry box*)
> Would you care for some pastry?

STEPHEN: Yeah, that'd be gre—
(*Stopping himself. Remembering he must be asked three
times*)
> No thanks. Just ate.

MASHKAN: So was it a woman or "Cavalleria Rusticana" and
"Der Bajazzo"?

STEPHEN: The operas.

MASHKAN: Und?

STEPHEN: Actually, I've never been a great fan of opera—
since there aren't many piano solos, but tonight, hearing
"Pagliacci"—

MASHKAN: Call it "Der Bajazzo," it means the clown. That's
what we call Pagliacci in Austria. And since we're in
Austria—

STEPHEN: "Der Bajazzo."

MASHKAN: Wonderful, ja?

STEPHEN (*coyly*): Not bad.

MASHKAN (*realizing Stephen is being coy, Mashkan perks up, getting into the spirit of the game*): You were crazy about it.

STEPHEN: It had its moments.

MASHKAN (*grabbing hat and putting it on his head*): Those costumes! The sets! More mammoth and awe-inspiring than you ever imagined, ja?
(*Seeing Stephen eyeing the pastry*)
Have a pastry.

STEPHEN (*remembering it's just the second time being asked*): . . . No, thanks.

MASHKAN: I'll bet your eyes popped out when the curtain went up!

STEPHEN (*still pretending to be blase*): If you like spectacle.

MASHKAN: And when the singers' voices filled the opera house!

STEPHEN (*sincerely*): Incredible.

MASHKAN: And the orchestra! The sound!

STEPHEN (*in awe*): Amazing! The power and richness behind those voices!

MASHKAN: I told you! I told you you would be bowled over!
Pastry?

STEPHEN (*not sure how many times he's been asked*): Uh,
that's okay.
(*Pretending to be indifferent*)
And I wouldn't say bowled over. I mean, I'll admit the
acoustics were exemplary.
(*Goading Mashkan*)
Must really be something to hear some good *modern
music* at the Staatsoper.

MASHKAN (*indignant*): Modern music?!

STEPHEN: You know, Philip Glass.

MASHKAN: The man who finds one melody and repeats it for
three hours!
(*Stephen is obviously enjoying Mashkan's tirade*)
Oh I see. Another of your feeble attempts at humor.
(*Both laugh. Mashkan holds out the pastry*)
For the *fourth* time.

STEPHEN: If you insist.
(*Taking out money*)
Twenty schillings.

MASHKAN (*getting up, a little dizzy*): I think I need some
more coffee. And you?

STEPHEN: Don't go to any trouble.

MASHKAN: It's already warming on the back-burner.

STEPHEN: Is it decaf?

MASHKAN (*exiting to kitchenette*): For once, you're not too tense. Go for the real thing!

(*Stephen goes to the piano and picks up the glass of whiskey. As he does, a crash is heard*)

STEPHEN: You okay?

MASHKAN (*offstage*): I dropped a cup. That's all.

STEPHEN: Need some help?

MASHKAN (*offstage*): I manage by myself. As always.

(*Stephen sits back down. He opens the pastry box*)

STEPHEN (*calling to Mashkan*): You should go to my pastry shop. They only charge sixteen schillings. It's just around the corner. It's called—
(*Stephen picks up the box and sees the name of his pastry shop on it. He says softly*)
Tabir.

MASHKAN (*offstage*): I didn't hear you. What's it called?

STEPHEN: . . . That's funny. All of a sudden, it's slipped my mind. . . . You know, Mashkan, for me the best part of the evening was the end. The clown, his life in shambles, cries "La comedia est finita!"

MASHKAN (*offstage*): Sadness and comedy all in one moment.

STEPHEN: And after that the curtain whooshed to the floor—it seemed to fall it flew down so fast.

MASHKAN (*reentering, carrying in coffee*): A man is 'specially trained to bring it down. That is his only task. A wonderful job.

STEPHEN (*puzzled*): Well, not quite as wonderful as a professor.

MASHKAN: More lucrative. And stable. It's hard to fire someone from a union job like that.

STEPHEN: Hard to fire someone with tenure, too.

MASHKAN: First one must hold a job long enough to get it.

STEPHEN: . . . You don't have tenure?

MASHKAN (*pouring coffee*): Careful. The coffee is hot. It may burn your tongue.

STEPHEN (*sipping it*): It's not hot.

MASHKAN: No? Then maybe I wasn't talking about the coffee.

(*They sip*)

STEPHEN: . . . When'd you start teaching again?

MASHKAN: Two . . . three weeks ago.

STEPHEN (*suddenly dawning on him*): Am I your only student? That doesn't seem possible. I mean, you're so in control of your life. So . . . strong.

MASHKAN: Ah strong. Like tonight's coffee. But why is it so strong? Because it has been simmering on the backburner, slowly evaporating away. In other words, it's strength comes from a part of it disappearing. (*Heartfelt*) A sad strength.

(*Beat*)

STEPHEN: I like my coffee strong. It gives me a rush. Same way I used to feel playing the piano.

MASHKAN: Used to? . . . Ah, so it's the Sitzfleisch you're currently lacking.
(*Stephen looks puzzled*)
It's the will to keep the seat of the pants sticking to the seat of the chair!

STEPHEN: Hmmm . . . I'm not sure I ever really had that . . . My mother has it. She's a painter. Spends hours over the most minute detail—the back of a hand. The shading of a leaf. And loves doing it. My father's a math professor. I'll bet he thinks math is better than sex. I play the piano. And I'm a superb—
(*Said derogatorily*)
technician.
(*Going to the piano*)
When I stopped giving concerts a year ago . . . I was

relieved. Sometimes I think the only reason I play is because it came so easily to me. It was a gift.

(*Running his hands over the keys, quickly playing ascending scales with both hands*)

I sat down when I was four and started playing Tchaikowsky's "Waltz in E Flat."

(*Stephen starts to play the waltz—without breathing or tugging—as he says*)

Everyone thought I was a prodigy. I wasn't. I was a mimic. I listened to the masters and duplicated what they played. Music didn't excite me. Pretending to be someone else—that was the kick. If I had to play something bold, yet romantic, say Liszt, I'd put on my Horowitz hat.

(*Putting on his hat—jauntily tilting it to the side, then playing some Liszt. He finishes, then says*)

For something more academic, very classical, very Beethoven, Alfred Brendel.

(*Shifting hat so it's perfectly upright, then playing Beethoven. Finishes, then says*)

When I'm immersing myself deep within Bach—without the pedal—Glenn Gould. And I even get to hum along.

(*Shifting hat—pulling it down, completely covering his face, then playing Bach. Finishes, then says*)

It was fun. Uncomplicated. . . .

(*Playing Tchaikowsky waltz again, although this time sweetly, sadly*)

Ah, to be nine forever.

MASHKAN: And why can't you be?

STEPHEN: And mimick my whole life? I want to feel something for once.

MASHKAN: You seemed to—playing a few weeks ago.

STEPHEN (*music stops*): True. . . . Or was I just temporarily wearing your hat?

MASHKAN: *My* artist's hat? Impossible. I don't have one. You see, I don't have a hat head. No great musical gift. I never woke when *I* was four and astounded the world.
(*Truly romantic, wistful*)
But if these pipes could sing. . . .
(*Snapping out*)
More coffee?

STEPHEN: Please.

(*There is an uncomfortable silence as both realize that Stephen has momentarily observed Mashkan's private world*)

MASHKAN: I knew you would love the Staatsoper!

STEPHEN (*agreeing*): Hmmm . . .
(*Teasing*)
even though it *is* an old building.

MASHKAN: So 1955 is considered old these days?

STEPHEN (*surprised*): How could that building be only—

MASHKAN: The original was destroyed during the war. It was completely rebuilt.

STEPHEN: All that effort—Why didn't they just put up a new one?

MASHKAN: Ah yes, that *was* foolish of them. But I suppose some people prefer to live in the past . . . Or maybe, perhaps, the original represented the heart of Vienna—and we needed to get it back.

STEPHEN (*really thinking that over*): . . . That makes sense.

MASHKAN (*amused*): Thank you.

(*Beat*)

STEPHEN: After I left the opera, I walked around—the streets were packed with people, a lot of them old—with great wrinkled faces. But so many in wheelchairs or crippled.

MASHKAN: World War II may be ancient history to you in the United States, but we still live with it everyday . . . I have often thought that if Vienna were a piano, World War II would be a delicate piano shawl—lightly draped over the whole city.

STEPHEN: Only lightly? I heard the Jewish population used to be over three hundred thousand. Now it's less than ten thousand. I mean *that* alone, hanging over Vienna—

MASHKAN: Why does everyone always harp on the Jews?! They are not the only ones who suffered!
(*Beat*)
I must be going. Are you having another pastry?

STEPHEN: No thanks.

MASHKAN: This time I am not being polite. I don't have enough money to get a cab home. But if you're having two more—

STEPHEN: I'm having three.

(*Stephen pays Mashkan*)

MASHKAN: See you Friday afternoon.

STEPHEN (*nervous*): Right. I was wondering. Could we make it a little earlier? I'm finally going to Munich, München, this weekend.

MASHKAN: Oh good! I will help plan your weekend for you.

STEPHEN: That's okay. Professor Schiller—
(*Suddenly wishing he hadn't said that*)
—said he'd let me know the hot spots.

MASHKAN (*uneasy*): . . . So you met with him?

STEPHEN: We spoke—on the phone. We meet Friday morning.

MASHKAN: You seem so pleased with my teaching one minute and then the next . . . well, after your meeting you will either be free of me or trapped in this hellhole for two more months. Which will it be? I wonder. Our Friday afternoon lesson should prove to be interesting. Lots of Sturm und Drang. Auf Wiedersehen, Stefan.

STEPHEN: Auf Wiedersehen, Mashkan.

MASHKAN: Thank you for going to the opera.

STEPHEN (*coldly*): Thanks for making me.

MASHKAN: You are very, very strange.

STEPHEN (*trying to be jovial*): And you like that.

(*Mashkan exits.*

Stephen goes back to the piano and tries to put on the Tyrolean hat—but he can't find a position that fits comfortably on his head.

He throws it off.

Stephen begins softly playing the last few sung bars of the aria "Vesti la Giubba"—specifically on the words "Ridi Pagliaccio" as the lights dim.)

End Scene Three

MUSICAL NOTE
Just before Stephen hit the final resolving chord of "Vesti la Giubba," the recorded music plays the fourth song of "Dichterliebe" (Wenn ich in deine Augen seh')—or the fifth song could also be used.

LIGHTING NOTE
Since the upcoming fourth scene of Act One will be full of "Sturm und Drang" including thunder and lightning, the

last 15 or so seconds of this scene change might foreshadow this with some darkly dramatic operatic lighting. Then, as we're about to fade into scene four, the lights could transition to "reality."

ACT I

Scene Four

SETTING: *Mashkan's studio. Friday afternoon. It's pouring outside.*

AT RISE: *Mashkan plays the last phrase of "Ich grolle nicht." The thunder crashes right after the song ends. Mashkan marvels at the coincidence. Then an o.s. knocking is heard.*

MASHKAN: Kommen sie herein.

(*Stephen enters dripping wet. He seems ill at ease. He has his suitcase with him*)

Why didn't you carry an umbrella?

STEPHEN (*holding up his destroyed umbrella*): I did.

MASHKAN: Let me take that. You were late. That is not like you. Did you—stop somewhere first?

STEPHEN (*changing the subject*): Where should I put my jacket?

MASHKAN: Anywhere. Ah, your suitcase. For München?

STEPHEN: Ja.

(*Stephen puts the wet jacket on the couch*)

MASHKAN: Not the couch.
(*Stephen puts it on the chair*)
Or the chair.

(As Stephen puts it on the piano)
I'll take it. It always seems to start raining on Friday, just before the weekend and finishes early Monday morning.

STEPHEN: I'm soaked . . . I don't know why I even came here. I've got a train to catch. I can only stay—ten minutes—at the most.

MASHKAN: Then why did you show up at all? . . . well, let us take advantage of what little time we have. . . . You look so serious. More than usual. Did anything happen—say, right before you came here? Maybe you bumped into someone? A professor, perhaps?

STEPHEN: I just have some things on my mind, that's all.

MASHKAN *(thinking he's about to be fired)*: Ja ja, no doubt. Drink your coffee. I have it waiting . . . while you sip, I'll talk—about our new song. . . . This piece is the only one in the "Dichterliebe," "the Poet's Love," where the singer has a chance to openly express his fury at being—
(Growing anger—thinking that Stephen has now met with Schiller)
deceived by his lover. The title itself "Ich Grolle Nicht"—
(Translating, said bitterly)
"I bear no grudge" . . . *This is a lie!* You can hear it in the music.
(Mashkan forcefully plays the opening)
ICH GROLLE NICHT
UND WENN DAS HERZ AUCH BRICHT

(*To Stephen*)
Translation.

STEPHEN: I bear no grudge although my heart may break.

MASHKAN: Yes.
(*Softly, almost lost in thought*)
Yes. . . .
(*Continuing on*)
This song, the accompanist must be 'specially aware of a singer's needs. The words are vital to the song. Their meaning must come through—above technical precision. Do not just play an incessant—
(*For a few bars, Mashkan plays the right hand rhythm. Then Mashkan stops*)
Now come, sing for me. Oh wait.
(*Mashkan gets up and loosens Stephen's tie. Stephen allows it*)
Better.

STEPHEN (*sings, as Mashkan plays*):
ICH GROLLE NICHT
UND WENN DAS HERZ AUCH BRICHT

MASHKAN: Your *heart*. Let us hear it!

STEPHEN (*following instructions throughout the song*):
EWIG VERLOR'NES LIEB

MASHKAN: Sadder.

STEPHEN: EWIG VERLOR'NES LIEB

MASHKAN: Now angrier.

STEPHEN: ICH GROLLE NICHT

MASHKAN: Angrier!

STEPHEN: ICH GROLLE NICHT

MASHKAN: Good breathing.

STEPHEN: WIE DU AUCH STRAHLST

MASHKAN: Stand straight!

STEPHEN: IN DIAMANTENPRACHT

MASHKAN: Remember how horrible she was!

STEPHEN (*trying, though still not enough emotion*):
ES FÄLLT KEIN STRAHL
IN DEINES HERZENS NACHT

MASHKAN: The ritard!

STEPHEN (*slowing down*): DAS WEISS

MASHKAN: More bitter!

STEPHEN: ICH LÄNGST

MASHKAN: Now I build, but you come in soft.

STEPHEN (*getting into it*):
ICH GROLLE NICHT
UND WENN DAS HERZ AUCH BRICHT
ICH SAH DICH JA IM TRAUME

(*Mashkan stops playing*)
    UND SAH DIE NACHT—

(*Stephen stops singing, surprised*)

MASHKAN: We should stop. I think my mind, too, is on other things. . . .
(*Trying to pull himself together*)
    You were good. You have obviously practiced. Still, some passion is missing. . . . Maybe it's time for us to talk—about München. I have written out a possible itinerary for you. Unless you have already rounded up some helpful hints.

STEPHEN (*as he takes out slip of paper*): From Professor Schiller.

MASHKAN: So I thought.
(*Suddenly angry*)
    That is why you seem so distracted!

STEPHEN: That's not it at all!

MASHKAN (*angry*): You told him you wanted to drop me—after all I've taught you! This job is all I have!
(*Wishing he hadn't said that*)
    Schiller granted your request, didn't he? I can tell by that soft, pitying look in your eyes. I knew it. Only three weeks ago, Schiller put his arms around me and said, "Mashkan, you are a wonderful teacher. Others turn their back on you, not Schiller." But now he has obviously found someone who will do it cheaper—trying to jew me out of a job—

STEPHEN: Don't! Wait a minute! Professor Schiller said he would prefer I not drop your class. He said I needed to find depth in my playing! That you were some wise philosopher and I was an arrogant kid who needed the wind knocked out of him!

MASHKAN (*surprised*): Really?
(*Recovering his composure*)
Well that is true.

STEPHEN: Still, Schiller said dropping this class was ultimately my decision. He said I should take the weekend and give him my answer on Monday. I agreed. But I also made it very clear what a wonderful teacher you are. And how much I need you to help me—find my way back.

MASHKAN (*modestly*): No. . . . Really? You told him that? . . .
(*Cocky*)
I *am* a good teacher. Have a pastry. On me. Only eighteen schillings. Some coffee?

STEPHEN: No thanks.

MASHKAN: I think *I'll* have some. For some reason, I'm suddenly hungry.
(*As Mashkan exits to kitchenette, he says*)
So what are your plans for München?

STEPHEN: I'm taking your advice. I'm going to experience joy and sadness. For the joy, I'm going to see "The Marriage of Figaro" and then get drunk at the beerhall. For the sadness I'm planning—

Hal Robinson (*left*) as Professor Josef Mashkan and
Justin Kirk as Stephen Hoffman.

*All photographs from the 1996 production at The Promenade Theatre
in New York City, by Carol Rosegg.*

Hal Robinson as Professor Josef Mashkan and
Justin Kirk as Stephen Hoffman.

Hal Robinson as Professor Josef Mashkan and
Justin Kirk as Stephen Hoffman.

Hal Robinson as Professor Josef Mashkan and
Justin Kirk as Stephen Hoffman.

(*Not wanting to admit it*)
   to go to Dachau—the concentration camp.

MASHKAN (*offstage*): Sure you don't want any coffee?

STEPHEN: No, I'm tense enough, thank you!

MASHKAN (*o.s.—calling to Stephen*): So you want to go to Dachau, you say?

STEPHEN (*uneasy*): That's right.

MASHKAN (*reentering*): Do not do that. Ja, it's sad, that is true. But we can find other sad things to send you to.
(*Trying to be humorous*)
   Besides, Dachau is just a bunch of dead Jews.

STEPHEN (*embarrassed to say this*): . . . You know that's the . . . the kind of remark that can get a teacher fired.

MASHKAN: What?

STEPHEN (*feeling uneasy*): I mean if you— . . . I'm Jewish.

MASHKAN (*puzzled*): But I thought you said you were Protestant.

STEPHEN: I lied.

MASHKAN: Why?

STEPHEN: I don't know. Maybe I was just trying on my Christian hat . . . I have to get out of here. I can't miss

61

this train. See, I made a deal with my Dad. He'd help pay for Vienna if I agreed to visit Dachau. And a deal's a deal.

(*Lightly pointed*)

And you know how we Jews love making our deals.

(*Stephen, his suitcase and coat in hand, leaves. Mashkan stands there, stunned.*

The moment the door slams behind Stephen, we hear recorded music of the last five thundering piano bars of "Ich grolle nicht." At the same time the stage quickly goes dark except for a spotlight on Mashkan.

After the final chord of "Ich grolle nicht" crashes down—blackout.)

End of Act One

ACT
II

ACT II

Scene One

TIME: *Tuesday morning, two weeks later.*

SETTING: *Mashkan's studio. Disheveled. Papers everywhere, empty cups of coffee.*

AT RISE: *Mashkan lies on the sofa, asleep, covered by a blanket. Silence.*

Mashkan screams and bolts upright on the couch.

Getting off the couch, he quickly rushes over to the clock to check the time. But then remembers that the clock is broken.

At this point we see that Mashkan's clothes are crumpled; his hair disheveled.

Mashkan goes to the piano and starts practicing "Ich grolle nicht."

A knocking at the door is heard.

Mashkan quickly begins straightening himself and the place up—throwing the blanket under the sofa, combing his hair, tucking in his shirt. As he does this he calls out:

MASHKAN (*in German*): Ja ja ja. Ein momenterl bitte!
(*Finally*)
    Kommen sie herein.
(*The knocking is heard again*)
    Kommen sie herein.

(*Knocking again*)
   Come in.
(*Stephen enters and stands by the door, silent, hostile*)
   Grüss Gott.

STEPHEN (*stern—with understated anger*): I'll greet him
   when I see him.

MASHKAN (*said very lightly*): . . . It's good to see you after
   only—what? Two—two and a half weeks? Have you
   been ill?

STEPHEN:
(*Silent*)

MASHKAN: Well, come in, come in.
(*Stephen walks further into the studio. He's wearing a light
jacket, sweat shirt and blue jeans*)
   I like your new clothes. Much easier to sing in.

(*Stephen circles the room. He stops as he looks at the clock*)

STEPHEN (*very calm*): Stuck, as always. It looks like both
   hands have drooped just about as low as possible, without the energy or strength of character to pull themselves back up.

MASHKAN (*puzzled*): I never thought of it that way.

STEPHEN: Ironic.

MASHKAN: Is it?

STEPHEN: You might say it represents Vienna. Trapped in a moment in time. But is it right before sunrise or the last gasp before sunset?

MASHKAN (*ignoring his words, said lightly*): . . . Why don't we start with a scale to warm up?

(*Mashkan heads toward the piano. Stephen beats him there, sits down, then softly plays the right hand melody to Strauss' "Tales From the Vienna Woods" without breathing or tugging. As he plays*)

STEPHEN: I walked around Vienna these last two weeks. It's all a lie. The Blue Danube isn't blue, it's brown! And it doesn't even run through the city. The Wien river does.

(*Stephen's left hand joins in*)

STEPHEN: The Ringstrasse running around the center of Vienna isn't a ring, but three quarters of a circle at most . . . St. Mary's on the Banks doesn't even lie on a bank! (*Now Stephen plays the beginning of the "B" section—four eighth notes, a half and a quarter*)
Your history books say you were forcibly invaded by the Germans, but in 1938 there were about half a million Austrian Nazis—proportionally more Nazis than in Germany.
(*Music continues*)
And only a few months ago Kurt Waldheim's campaign slogan was "A man whom the world trusts!"

(*End song*)

MASHKAN: Obviously, you are warmed up. Shall we sing?

STEPHEN (*standing up*): You haven't asked about my trip to Munich.

MASHKAN: First let us practice "Ich grolle nicht." You *have* practiced, haven't you? You have not disappointed me?

STEPHEN: I haven't. Although I'm not sure what the Dichterliebe—"the Poet's Love"—has to do with life.

MASHKAN (*slipping onto the piano bench*): That is *my* job to show you. And now, "Ich grolle nicht". . . . Ja?

STEPHEN: And then we talk.
(*Mashkan starts playing "Ich Grolle Nicht." Stephen sings*)
  I HATE—YOU NOT

(*Mashkan stops playing*)

MASHKAN: You're singing in English.

STEPHEN (*too innocently*): Am I?

MASHKAN: It's written in German.

STEPHEN (*matter-of-factly*): But I'm no longer speaking German.

MASHKAN: How are we to do the song?

STEPHEN: You tell me. Or should I leave?

MASHKAN: . . . Why don't you sing it in English?

(*Mashkan begins playing again*)

STEPHEN (*sings*): I HATE YOU NOT

MASHKAN (*stops playing again*): The translation is "I bear no grudge." Those are the words.

STEPHEN: But not the feelings. Stop being so literal. Allow me some artistic license.
(*Mashkan begins playing again. Stephen sings with great personal intensity and impeccable musicianship*)
   I HATE—YOU NOT
   ALTHOUGH MY HEART MAY BREAK
   LOVE IS FOREVER LOST
   LOVE IS FOREVER LOST
   I HATE YOU NOT
(*Directed at Mashkan*)
   I HATE YOU NOT

MASHKAN (*understated*): Nice anger.

STEPHEN:
   THOUGH YOU MAY GLOW
   IN DIAMONDS SPARKLING BRIGHT

MASHKAN: Pushing too hard.

STEPHEN:
   INSIDE YOUR HEART
   THERE IS JUST DARK—NOT LIGHT
(*Slowing down*)
   THIS I KNOW WELL

MASHKAN: That's it! Take control of the song!

STEPHEN (*coming in early*):
I HATE YOU NOT

MASHKAN: Too much control! Wait for me!

STEPHEN (*plowing on, forcing Mashkan to keep catching up*):
ALTHOUGH MY HEART MAY BREAK
I SEE YOU WHEN I'M DREAMING
I SEE A HEART THAT'S COLD AND
  UNREDEEMING

MASHKAN: Slow down.

STEPHEN (*continuing on*):
WHERE ONCE A HEART
I SEE THERE'S NOW A SCAR
I SEE MY LOVE HOW TRULY LOST YOU ARE

I HATE YOU NOT
I HATE YOU—NOT.

(*End song*)

MASHKAN (*thrilled*): The translation is loose, but the intent—and the anger: Gut! But what happened to that perfect inner metronome?

STEPHEN: I sang with my feelings.

MASHKAN: And completely ignored the beat. It was all you, you, you. What about the piano?

STEPHEN: *You're* supposed to follow *me*.

MASHKAN: But you must be aware of my musicianship, give me my moments, allow us to blend, to become one.

STEPHEN: And what if I don't agree with your interpretation?

MASHKAN: Common ground must exist.

STEPHEN:
(*Silent*)

MASHKAN (*slyly*): Pastry?

STEPHEN: Thank you.

(*Mashkan hands him a pastry. Stephen takes a bite*)

MASHKAN: Ah, you forgot to—

STEPHEN: They only cost 16 schillings. I shop at the same store. But I'll pay 20. I don't want you to think I'm cheap.
(*Mashkan is silent. Stephen pays*)
You still haven't asked me about my trip to Munich.

MASHKAN: This pastry seems tart today.

STEPHEN: How can we find common ground in our music if you don't try to understand me as a person?

MASHKAN: Your music communicates all I need to know.

(*Beat*)

STEPHEN: Aren't you going to offer me coffee?

MASHKAN: You think I'm crazy?!

(*Stephen laughs, then stops himself*)

STEPHEN (*serious again*): Two weeks ago, I took the train to Munich. The next morning I took another train from Munich to Dachau—

MASHKAN: I do not want—

STEPHEN: —I arrived at the station fairly early, assuming the ride would take a while. It took twenty minutes. Isn't that interesting? Only twenty minutes from the heart of Munich to Dachau.

MASHKAN: I think *I'll* have some coffee.

STEPHEN: At first, I thought I was on the wrong train. So I turned to an older woman sitting next to me and asked her in German if this was the way to Dachau.

MASHKAN: Actually, if you'd like some coffee—

STEPHEN: And she said to me "I knew nothing that went on there!"

From the train, I took a short bus ride to the camp. On the bus, a young woman in front of me turned around and said "What are you doing here?!" I told her, "I'm here to see Dachau." She asked me "why?" and I said (*stammering*) "because it's important for people to see this place." And she said, "but why do *you* want to see it?!" And I said: "because I'm Jewish." And then she said,

(*very casually*)

"well why didn't you say so in the first place?"

Then she told me to move over—and sat next to me. Her name was Sarah. She grew up in Israel. Her grandparents had been in Dachau. They didn't want her to see it . . . Together, she and I did.

It's funny. I was prepared for the "Arbeit Macht Frei" sign, the barbed wire fences, the guard posts. I *wasn't* prepared for how beautifully Dachau had been fixed up. No, covered over. Most of the buildings—gone. Those that were left—whitewashed. The grass—so green. A stream near the side of the camp had a quaint little bridge. If I hadn't known better, I'd never suspect these few acres of land had been crowded with thousands of emaciated, tortured bodies.

There was a small museum which told "the story"— mostly through pictures. And under each picture, a description. The only problem—the descriptions were in German—*no* translations. So most people there couldn't read it since German was not the predominant language among visitors. For those of us who could read the captions, they supplied only the barest of facts.

As I walked through, I was silent. Stunned. Feeling— numb from the experience. Not Sarah. She was enraged. I could see her whole body tightening up as we walked from room to room in the museum. Finally, we passed a guard and she started yelling at him, saying he was burying the truth! . . . And the whole time he just stood there expressionless—silent.

After that, we saw the crematorium. Sarah cried. I couldn't. I was too angry. And confused.

Before leaving, we saw the Israeli Memorial. It's a stone tower. You look into it by going down a ramp and peering through a gate. Inside, its almost completely dark except for a small beam of light that shines down from the top . . . a single beam of light surrounded by darkness . . . You can't go inside the memorial. The gate's locked.

On the way out of the camp, we picked up a brochure—*this* one in English—telling us to "please stroll through the lovely *town* of Dachau after leaving." We didn't. For some reason, the Bavarian charm was lost on us.

That evening, we spent a quiet dinner together. At the end of the main course, Sarah asked if I would spend the night with her.

Back at her hotel room we made love.
(*Surprised, embarrassed*)
It was hot. Really hot. For hours and hours into the night. And then again the next morning. And I kept thinking, "why is this so special? Because she's Jewish? Or because of what happened at Dachau? Or is she just great in bed?" Or am I suddenly better in bed? And then it hit me—
(*Not pleased*)

You were right. That combination of sadness and joy. With one emotion heightened, so is the other.

The next afternoon, she caught her train to Prague.

And these last two weeks, I've wandered through Vienna, "the city of dreams." And everytime I turned and saw a beautiful bridge or a quaint babbling brook, I broke into a sweat. And everytime I got off the U-bahn and heard that recorded message "End of the line, everybody off," I felt sick to my stomach. And thought of a man I had respected. Once.

(*Stephen starts gathering up his music*)

MASHKAN: I listened to your story!
(*Stephen drops his Tyrolian hat in front of Mashkan*)
　　Please, do not turn this into some kind of overly tragic Viennese melodrama.

STEPHEN (*re: the hat*): It doesn't fit me after all.

(*Stephen continues gathering his things together to go*)

MASHKAN: You are making so much progress. Finally getting some passion into your life. And your music. This is the kind of Stefan I wanted to see! Professor Schiller will thank me!
(*Stephen starts for the door*)
　　For whatever we had, give me one minute of your time. . . . Please.
(*Stephen stops*)
　　Sit.

(*Stephen doesn't*)
Have you followed the election for president?

STEPHEN: What does this—

MASHKAN: Again, you Americans want immediate results!
Allow me a chance.

STEPHEN: . . . I'm listening.

(*Mashkan begins rolling up his right hand sleeve*)

MASHKAN (*speaking very casually, half-amused*): I do not
know what all the fuss is over Waldheim. When the
government was run by Kreisky—who wouldn't even
admit he was a Jew—he recruited politicians with as
much of a past as Waldheim. At least four ex-Nazis and
one S.S. officer. You can't run a country so heavily Nazi
without hiring a few. So what's the fuss with
Waldheim?!

(*Stephen sees there is a concentration camp number tat-
tooed on Mashkan's arm*)

STEPHEN: Oh God.

(*As Stephen sits, shocked, Mashkan continues speaking*)

MASHKAN (*lightly, animated*): I am sure Waldheim will win.
And when he does, the Viennese can make bets on
which countries will refuse to greet him. It will be quite
a bit of fun. That's what I think!
(*Silence as Mashkan rolls his sleeve back down, covering
up the tattoo. Then Mashkan says drolly*)

So you see, Stefan, once again your American mind assumed the obvious—that I was a Nazi. Life is not so clearcut. There is a mind inside of there. Make it work!

STEPHEN (*confused*): But to say Dachau was just a bunch of dead Jews?

MASHKAN (*again lightly*): Disgraceful. And do you know how many times I have heard it said by intelligent Viennese men and women? . . . this is why I say anti-Jewish comments first—before anyone else has the chance. My words sting, but not quite as sharply as theirs . . . "Ich grolle nicht, und wenn das Herz auch bricht"—"I bear no grudge—although my heart may break."

STEPHEN (*not realizing the rudeness of his question*): Where were you sent? I mean which camp?

MASHKAN (*amused*): Ah, you want to know "my story." No . . . each person has but one story in him. Tell it to everyone and its meaning is cheapened.

For next week, practice the eighth song in the "Dichterliebe." It begins: "Und wüssten's die Blumen die kleinen—
(*Lightly sings the rest*)
WIE TIEF VERWUNDENT MEIN HERZ
SIE WÜRDEN MIT MIR WEINEN
(*Translating*)
If the flowers knew of my grief, they would weep.

STEPHEN: I won't sing it in German.

MASHKAN (*tongue-in-cheek*): And I will not play the piano in
   German.

(*And as the lights swiftly fade. . . .*)

End Scene One

MUSICAL NOTE
*In darkness, we hear a recorded version of the eighth song
of the "Dichterliebe": "Und wüssten's die Blumen, die
kleinen."*

LIGHTING NOTE
*A few seconds into hearing this song, lights come up half-
way and the room appears almost in a haze, as if we're in a
semi-real, extremely private moment that we somehow feel
we shouldn't quite be privy to. We see Mashkan, who's
been drinking, listening to the gramophone. The eighth
song switches from the house speakers to coming directly
from Mashkan's gramophone.*

*As he listens to the music of "Und wüssten's die Blumen,
die kleinen" ("And if the flowers knew"), he looks around at
his mementos.*

*He takes a liquor bottle and sets it down on the coffee table
as lights fade.*

ACT II

Scene Two

SETTING: *Mashkan's studio. The next Friday.*

AT RISE: *Mashkan lies on the couch. Asleep. There is a knock at the door. Then another. Mashkan doesn't move.*

Using his key, Stephen opens the door. He wears a yarmulke.

Stephen doesn't see Mashkan because the couch faces away from him.

STEPHEN (*calling out*): Mashkan?
(*Seeing him asleep on the couch*)
 Sleeping on the job.

(*Stephen stands there a moment, not sure if he should leave and let Mashkan sleep.*

Stephen goes to Mashkan, rolls up his sleeve, and looks at the numbers on his arm, fascinated. He touches the numbers one by one.

Suddenly, Mashkan stirs.

Stephen quickly drops his hand. And for the first time notices a glass of whiskey on the table and an empty bottle of pills. He picks it up.

Stephen smells Mashkan's breath and starts shaking him)

Mashkan. Mashkan! Wake up!

79

MASHKAN (*waking up, almost jumping up out the couch*):
Where's the fire?!

STEPHEN: What are these pills?! What did you take?!
(*Mashkan doesn't respond; he's in his own agitated world*)
Mashkan, how many did you take?!

MASHKAN (*to himself, angry, high and very much awake*):
Forty-three! . . . Forty-four!

STEPHEN (*looking at bottle*): You can't even fit forty-four in
here. How many did you take?!

MASHKAN (*almost laughing, giddy*): Forty-five!

STEPHEN: Mashkan!

MASHKAN (*finally noticing Stephen*): Oh hello.

STEPHEN: The pills! We're going to have to throw them up!
Do you hear me?!

MASHKAN: You do it and tell me how it went.

STEPHEN: This is no time to joke!

(*Stephen tries pulling Mashkan to the bathroom*)

MASHKAN: Where are we going?

STEPHEN: To the bathroom.

MASHKAN (*overly dramatic*): Not me. I'm lying here and
dying.

STEPHEN (*going to the phone*): I'm calling an ambulance. What's the number?!

MASHKAN (*giddy*): Actually, I'm not dying. That's my punishment!

STEPHEN: What is the number?!
(*Going back and shaking Mashkan*)
Mashkan, *what is the NUMBER?!*

(*Beat*)

MASHKAN (*matter-of-fact, as if Stephen were an idiot*): It's written on the phone.
(*As a petrified Stephen races over and dials, Mashkan speaks*)
I wrote it there myself. I have excellent handwriting—when I want to. My mother taught me calligraphy . . . May she rest in peace—as you Americans say. I like that expression. "Rest in peace."

STEPHEN (*in German, on the phone*): Ich brauche eine Ambulanz! [I need an ambulance!]

MASHKAN: No! No German! You were right!

STEPHEN (*in German*): Ein Mann hat sich vergiftet! [A man has taken an overdose.]

MASHKAN: Only English!

STEPHEN (*to Mashkan*): She won't understand—
(*Into phone, in German*)
Hallo? . . . Ja, ein Mann hat sich vergiftet. . . .

Nein, ich kann ihn nicht zum Erbrechen bringen. . . .
Ja, ich verstehe. . . . Professor Josef Mashkan. Er
wohnt bei. . . . Sicher. . . . Danke.

[Hello? . . . Yes, a man has taken an overdose. . . .
No, I can't get him to throw it up. . . . Yes, I under-
stand. . . . Professor Josef Mashkan. He's over on.
. . . That's right. . . . Thank you.]
(*To Mashkan, still in German*)
Sie kommen schon herüber. [They're coming over.]

MASHKAN: English!

STEPHEN (*in English*): They'll be right here. . . . You can
thank me later.

MASHKAN: Yes, please remind me.
(*Stephen starts pulling at Mashkan's bow tie*)
What are you doing?!

STEPHEN: Loosening your tie.

MASHKAN: . . . For proper breathing!
(*Mashkan allows it. Then Stephen starts pulling Mashkan
up from the couch*)
Now what are you doing?!

STEPHEN: They said to keep you moving.
(*Stephen continues pulling Mashkan up. Mashkan doesn't
move*)
Well give me a little help!

(*Beat*)

MASHKAN: Okay.
(*Mashkan suddenly and almost effortlessly gets up. Stephen is stunned.*

Stephen and Mashkan then circle the room throughout the rest of the scene. Although Mashkan isn't always feeling well, he remains wide awake and often giddy)

STEPHEN: Why did you do this?!

MASHKAN: Turn your head.
(*Stephen turns*)
   You have a black smudge on it.

STEPHEN: It's a yarmulke.

MASHKAN: Why are you wearing it? Have you suddenly gone religious?!

STEPHEN: It's time Vienna saw some Jews who were proud of their heritage.

MASHKAN: Wearing it to make a statement. Don't believe what it stands for. Sacrilege! No different than speaking German when you despise it. Take it off!

STEPHEN: I will not.

MASHKAN: I am asking you to!
(*Mashkan moans and holds his stomach*)
   Oh. Oooh.

STEPHEN: Are you all right?
(*Mashkan continues holding his stomach*)
    Mashkan?! . . . Tell me what to do!

MASHKAN (*simple sincerity*): Hold me.

(*Stephen, not used to physically reaching out to others, very gingerly holds Mashkan.*)

Beat—as Mashkan continues breathing heavily for a moment, being held by Stephen.

Mashkan, having somewhat faked the pain in his stomach, suddenly grabs Stephen's yarmulke from his head)

    Got it!
(*Pointing to yarmulke*)
    If you don't feel it on the inside, don't wear it on the outside!

STEPHEN: Give me back my yarmulke!

MASHKAN (*very professional*): Keep me moving. Shirking your job.
(*Stephen continues walking Mashkan*)
    Finally able to hold me. To touch. You are becoming almost human.
(*Stephen tries to grab the yarmulke from Mashkan's hand*)
    What are you doing?!

STEPHEN: Give it back. Don't make me fight with a dying man!

MASHKAN: I told you—I am living forever!

STEPHEN: Not if I don't get that yarmulke back!

MASHKAN (*very serious*): That is a terrible thing to say.

(*They continue circling*)

STEPHEN (*feeling bad*): You're right. Keep the yarmulke.

MASHKAN: You give in too easily. I was only kidding.

(*As they continue circling*)

STEPHEN: What's taking them so long?

MASHKAN: You *just* called.

STEPHEN: After I told the ambulance your name, I didn't have to give the address. They knew it.

MASHKAN (*tongue-in-cheek*): It's good to have people who know you.

STEPHEN: Is that why you can't hold on to a job? Because you keep trying to commit suicide?

MASHKAN: Apparently, these attempts make me appear unstable. Go figure.

STEPHEN: What provoked it today? Couldn't be anything I said, could it?
(*Realizing it might have been, Stephen smacks his head hard the way he did earlier and says*)
I can't do anything right!

85

MASHKAN: Careful! You almost dropped me!

(*As they walk*)

STEPHEN: So is this the forty-third, fourth or fifth time you've tried to kill yourself?

MASHKAN: Not quite so many.

STEPHEN: Then those numbers?

MASHKAN: Those numbers? Those are the years—
(*Mashkan suddenly holds his stomach in pain and turns to Stephen—serious*)
    Stefan—

STEPHEN: I'm ahead of you. Twenty steps we'll be in the bathroom. Just hold on.

(*They walk towards it. Mashkan suddenly stops*)

MASHKAN (*holding out yarmulke, tongue-in-cheek*): Take it. Just in case you feel the urge to pray for me.

(*And as the lights swiftly fade*)

End Scene Two

MUSICAL NOTE
Recorded music of the final section of the eighth song of the "Dichterliebe": "Und wüssten's die Blumen, die kleinen" is heard. As the song finishes. . . .

ACT II

Scene Three

SETTING: *Mashkan's studio. Hours later. Night.*

AT RISE: *Mashkan is on a chair, under a blanket.*

STEPHEN (*offstage*): Ready for your present?

MASHKAN: My what?
(*Stephen comes out of kitchenette with a huge stack of pastries piled up high on a tray*)
You should *not* have.

STEPHEN: I'm charging you for them.

MASHKAN: Then you *really* should not have.

STEPHEN: You need to get some food back in your stomach—although I'm not sure pastries. . . .

MASHKAN: Please, you are not my doctor. I am fine.
(*Taking a pastry*)
A stomach pump is an amazing thing. A machine spews out all the nastiness in your belly. If only there was a brain pump.

(*Stephen cleans up and looks at newspapers*)

STEPHEN: While your stomach was being pumped I read the papers. The race is close. Make sure you vote next month. I'll take you there myself.

MASHKAN: Waldheim will win whether I vote or not. . . .
And please, I am not a child. I can go to the polls by
myself.
(*Waiting for his coffee*)
Mein Kaffee.

STEPHEN: You just spoke German.

MASHKAN (*mock surprise*): Did I? . . . Well, what can one
do?

STEPHEN: You agreed you shouldn't.

MASHKAN: I believe I was in the middle of a suicide. I may
not have been completely right in the head. Besides,
German is my language as much as the Nazis'. When
you sing the "Dichterliebe," the words are by Heinrich
Heine, a great Jewish poet.

STEPHEN: Still . . . I'm not speaking it.

MASHKAN: You did. Phoning up the ambulance.

STEPHEN: —to save your life.

MASHKAN: And you took off your yarmulke when the ambulance arrived.

STEPHEN: I wanted you to have the best medical care.

MASHKAN: Oh and they would gas me if they thought I was
a Jew!

STEPHEN: You're overexerting yourself. Shut up.

MASHKAN: Your bedside manner stinks!
(*Still without coffee*)
  And thank you for the coffee.

STEPHEN: You were arguing with me—made me forget what I was doing!

MASHKAN: Always blaming others. . . . Come help me up.

STEPHEN: What for?

MASHKAN: Always, you must know everything. I think you enjoy controlling me. You are a control fiend.

STEPHEN: You're the one who tried to choose his own destiny. Can't get more controlling than that. And you know, if you'd died, your story would've died with you!

MASHKAN: This again. I do not just tell it to everyone.

STEPHEN: I'm not just everyone. I'm someone.

MASHKAN: Well, I do not just tell it to someone.

STEPHEN: I'll pass it to my children. They'll pass it to theirs.

MASHKAN: Sounds too Biblical for my taste. Besides, why do *you* want to know my story?!

STEPHEN (*sincerely*): . . . I told you *my* secrets. That's what friends do for each other . . . At least that's what I've read.

MASHKAN (*wryly*): . . . Friends. I see. . . . My secrets. You want me to say them? . . . The words. You have heard them before. Everyone has. They have become so commonplace. I'm sorry I cannot. . . . And now, please help me up. I want to look out the window.

(*Stephen helps Mashkan up. Mashkan still seems weak. As he heads for the window, he gets near the piano*)

Wait. Let me rest. On the piano bench.

(*As Mashkan sits on the piano bench, he pushes Stephen to the music stand and immediately begins playing "Am leuchtenden Sommermorgen"*)

STEPHEN (*stunned he's been tricked again*): What are you doing?!

MASHKAN (*stronger*): Lesson time! You missed this afternoon's.

STEPHEN: When you're stronger.

MASHKAN: I may be dead tomorrow.

STEPHEN: *You* said you'd never die.

MASHKAN: You listen too much. I am playing "Am leuchtenden Sommermorgen." "One Bright Summer Morning." These words, as well, are very familiar. So familiar they have become almost trite. In order to counter this, Schumann makes the music simple in its beauty.

And when the flowers sing "sei uns'rer Schwester nicht böse"—

(*music stops*)

"be not angry with our sister"—it is double piano. Very softly and from the heart. The sincerity of your voice must convince the man to be forgiving.

STEPHEN (*still angry*): Who are these flowers—demanding forgiveness?!

MASHKAN: They are not forcing it. Only trying to guide the man toward it.

STEPHEN: I think it's presumptuous!

MASHKAN (*puzzled at his anger*): Well . . . they're only flowers. What do they know?

(*Starts to play, then stops*)

Oh, and on this particular bright summer morning, as you walk through the garden, it's a very specific kind of walk. "Wandeln."

STEPHEN (*matter of fact; he knows it all*): Wandering.

MASHKAN: Not precisely. It's a little more—specific.

(*Standing, demonstrating*)

It's walking without focusing. Seeing, but not really seeing. Hearing without really hearing . . . Think about it while you sing.

(*Mashkan goes to piano*)

STEPHEN: And after that you'll tell me your story?!

MASHKAN (*ignoring him as he plays the piano, getting lost in the music*): Concentrate. Seeing without . . . seeing.

STEPHEN (*singing. Watching Mashkan getting lost in the music inspires him to do the same*):
ONE BRIGHT SHINING SUMMER MORNING

MASHKAN (*surprised*): Good start. Now go deeper inside yourself.

STEPHEN (*more lost in thought*):
AROUND THE GARDEN I WALK

MASHKAN (*half to himself, starting to despair*): Yes. Completely isolated. In your own private . . .

STEPHEN (*doing it more*):
THE FLOWERS CONVERSE IN A WHISPER

MASHKAN (*completely to himself, sadly*): That's it.

STEPHEN: BUT I REFUSE
(*Pointedly—to Mashkan*)
TO TALK!

MASHKAN (*dryly*): . . . Still pushing a little too much—but definitely coming along. Translating songs to English makes you more aware of the meaning. I will use this method on all my English speaking students. If ever I get any.

STEPHEN (*softly*): You will.

(*Mashkan's touched by Stephen's sweetness, though he doesn't say a word*)

MASHKAN: Also, be aware of the syncopation. You will find this same rhythm echoed in the final piano solo at the end of the "Dichterliebe."

STEPHEN (*not entirely paying attention—listening without really listening. Instead Stephen focuses on different things around Mashkan's room, searching for signs of "the story" as he replies*): I'll be on the lookout.

MASHKAN: Only then the music will be inspirational, rather than mournful as it is now. Are you listening, Stefan?

STEPHEN (*snapping out of it*): Stephen!

MASHKAN: No respect! . . . I like that. Yell at me. I am not some delicate French art song. I am strong like German lieder!

STEPHEN (*with controlled anger*): How can you compare yourself to something German after what they did to you?

MASHKAN: . . . So much anger.

Have you noticed this song brings us to a new season? And for the Poet, not a happy one.

(*Mashkan begins playing "Am leuchtenden Sommermorgen"—then stops*)

If you understate the grief, we will feel it all the more.

93

STEPHEN (*with clenched teeth, mocking Mashkan's instructions*):
ONE BRIGHT SHINING SUMMER MORNING
AROUND THE GARDEN I WALK. . . .

(*And as the lights fade*)

End Scene Three

MUSICAL NOTE
*The recorded music of "Am leuchtenden Sommermorgen"
sweeps in and takes over the live piano playing and singing.*

ACT II

Scene Four

SETTING: *Mashkan's studio. Tuesday, June 10, 1986.*

AT RISE: *The apartment has half a dozen newspapers and magazines lying out. Stephen and Mashkan are looking out the window. Mashkan's laughing.*

STEPHEN: The fat guy with the limp!

MASHKAN: No, the big-bosomed woman pushing the baby carriage!

STEPHEN: But look at the scowl on the fat guy's face!

MASHKAN: . . . Maybe both of them.

STEPHEN: I never thought of that.

MASHKAN: Well, since he won fifty-four percent of the vote, we know—

STEPHEN (*interrupting*): —*one* of them had to vote for Waldheim.

MASHKAN (*looking out window*): Ah, over there! Three nuns. . . . How many do you think?

STEPHEN/MASHKAN (*each to themselves*): All three.

(*Mashkan sighs, moving from window*)

STEPHEN: You're letting it get to you, again.

MASHKAN (*tongue-in-cheek*): And of course, there's no point getting depressed—since you threw away my pills!

STEPHEN: You said you knew Waldheim would win.

MASHKAN: That doesn't mean I believed it! . . . Even Waldheim's opponents didn't bring up his past. They thought it might lose them votes.

And I thought life was so complicated. It is very clearcut.

(*Beat*)

STEPHEN (*trying to change the subject*): I've been working on the new song.

MASHKAN: Turn your head. . . . Where's your "Look at me, I'm a Jew" hat?

STEPHEN: It kept falling off. I decided that was a sign from God. But from now on, when someone says something offensive, I'm speaking up!

MASHKAN: Another angry Jew. Just what the world needs.

(*Stephen stands in front of the piano, waiting for his lesson*)

Yes?

STEPHEN: Aren't we going to sing?

MASHKAN: You actually want to?

STEPHEN: Yes.

MASHKAN: Then *I* don't.

STEPHEN: The song seems pretty straightforward. I think it's the easiest one so far.

MASHKAN: Have you learned nothing? It's the most difficult. . . . And why?

STEPHEN (*trying to think fast*): Uh. . . . there's the repetition of the words "I weep bitterly" from the fourth song?

MASHKAN: Yes, we now have a greater understanding of his sadness, but more than that. . . .

STEPHEN (*thinking he has it*): Musically, the opening melody is the same as the second song, except down a minor third!

MASHKAN: These are just technical things.

STEPHEN: . . . I don't know.

MASHKAN: Well that's a first. Stefan Hoffman admits he does not know everything. Progress!

STEPHEN: So what's the answer?

(*Mashkan is silent*)

MASHKAN: See?

STEPHEN: No.

(*Again Mashkan is silent*)

I don't get what you're doing—

MASHKAN: Shhh. What do you hear? Silence. One of the most difficult things to feel comfortable with. And to allow to grow. Only in silence do we truly listen and comprehend.
(*Mashkan sits at the piano*)
In the first two verses you sing; then silence; then I play; silence; you sing, and so on. We must truly hear each other in order to have a growing dialogue. Both of us must take in what the other says, think about it, then respond. Only during the third verse will we come together and there is true understanding.

(*Mashkan plays a note*)

STEPHEN (*sings with sensitivity and accomplished musicianship*):
I WEPT WHILE I WAS DREAMING
(*Mashkan plays his accompaniment. Stephen comes in a little early*)
I DREAMT—

MASHKAN: Not so fast. Think about my music. I'm trying to lighten your grief. Let my lightheartedness resonate.

(*Mashkan plays his passage again*)

STEPHEN:
I DREAMT YOU WERE LYING IN A GRAVE

(*Mashkan doesn't play for a moment, thinking about the words. Then he plays*)

MASHKAN: I've listened to your words so my accompaniment this time isn't quite so glib. Now you try to be a tad lighter for me.

STEPHEN: WHEN I AWOKE

(*Mashkan plays accompaniment*)

MASHKAN: A little hopeful.

STEPHEN: I WAS CRYING

(*Mashkan plays accompaniment*)

MASHKAN: Less hopeful.

STEPHEN:
TEARS WERE STREAMING DOWN IN WAVES

MASHKAN: Fermata over the silence. Hear the tears streaming down.

STEPHEN (*he hears them, then sings*):
I WEPT WHILE I WAS DREAMING

MASHKAN (*instead of playing accompaniment, speaks*): You asked why I kept muttering 43, 44, and 45? Those are the years I remember almost nothing.

(*Mashkan plays his accompaniment*)

STEPHEN (*sings, although unsure if he should*):
I DREAMT YOU WERE LEAVING ME

MASHKAN: Who wants to remember a starving bunkmate pleading for bread? I turn away. He must not have a face. I do not want a friend. If he dies—*I* must face the loss, not him.
(*Lightly*)
Who needs more depression? I am already in a concentration camp.
(*Mashkan plays his accompaniment. Stephen is silent, not sure what to do*)
Keep singing! Try to be hopeful.

STEPHEN (*uneasy*):
WHEN I AWOKE

MASHKAN: And so I survive. Not because of my courage or compassion, but because I think only of myself.

(*Mashkan plays accompaniment*)

STEPHEN: I WAS CRYING

MASHKAN: Perhaps I will never die. For after each attempted suicide, I become more like that boiling coffee on the stove—growing stronger and stronger—and more and more bitter.

(*Mashkan plays accompaniment*)

STEPHEN: I CRIED SO BITTERLY

MASHKAN (*sings, the same words but in German, coming from the depth of his soul*): NOCH LANGE BITTER-LICH!
(*Mashkan plays cadence after phrase, then spoken*)
And now the music and the lyrics finally come together.

(*Mashkan plays again*)

STEPHEN (*heartfelt emotion*):
I WEPT WHILE I WAS DREAMING
I DREAMED YOU STILL CARED FOR ME
THEN I AWOKE
I WAS CRYING
MY TEARS KEPT FLOWING FREE

(*Mashkan plays accompaniment*)

MASHKAN: 1940. We were told to pack whatever we could fit into a suitcase.

STEPHEN (*very uneasy, not sure he wants to hear*): You don't have to tell me—

MASHKAN: Listen . . . It was spring—in the loveliest of months—May.
(*Sarcastic*)
"Im wunderschönen Monat Mai"
(*Recorded music of "Im wunderschönen Monat Mai" is softly heard*)
When all the buds were bursting in bloom—

(*As Mashkan leans into Stephen, the lights dim. Mashkan speaks, but no words are heard coming from his mouth.*

Instead we only hear the music of the "Dichterliebe" growing in volume.

Stephen nods, listening carefully to what Mashkan says. As the lights continue to dim, a single beam of light—just like the one described in the Israeli Memorial at Dachau [a single beam of light surrounded by darkness]—shines on Stephen.

Stephen stands—nodding and listening. Stephen starts to tear up. He tries not to cry. But does. Then sobs)

End Scene Four

MUSICAL NOTE

As Stephen listens, we hear the entire first song of the "Dichterliebe"—"Im wunderschönen Monat Mai." As the song ends, lights fade to black.

In darkness we hear the last song of the "Dichterliebe"— "Die alten, bösen Lieder". . . . Recorded music then segues to Mashkan playing the piano [starting on the pick-up notes to Bar 32 of this song]. As Mashkan continues playing, lights up on . . .

ACT II

Coda

SETTING: *Mashkan's studio. An early summer morning.*

AT RISE: *Mashkan plays "Die alten, bosen Lieder." Then Stephen and Mashkan sing.*

MASHKAN/STEPHEN (*near the end of the song, with energy*):
DIE SOLLEN DEN SARG FORTTRAGEN
UND SENKEN INS MEER HINAB!
DENN SOLCHEM GROSSEN SARGE
GEBÜHRT EIN GROSSES GRAB!

WISST IHR, WARUM DER SARG WOHL
SO GROSS UND SCHWERMAG SEIN?
(*Only Stephen takes the high note on "Sein"*)
ICH SENKT' AUCH MEINE LIEBE
UND MEINEN SCHMERZ HINEIN

(*Mashkan stops playing*)

MASHKAN: Before the final bars of the "Dichterliebe," the Andante espressivo, let us translate the song. I suppose this will be the last translation I hear from you.

STEPHEN: Professor Schiller's studio is only around the corner. We'll still see each other.

MASHKAN: I may not have time for you—my new students arrive next week. I am excited. They are Korean . . . Oh, have you heard the newest joke going around Vienna?

STEPHEN: I don't think so.

MASHKAN: Then I will tell you. You know of Alzheimer's disease, ja?

STEPHEN: Ja.

MASHKAN: Apparently, there is a new disease called Waldheimers. You get old—and forget you were a Nazi!

(*Mashkan laughs*)

STEPHEN: That's not funny.

MASHKAN (*still chuckling*): I know!
(*Truly serious*)
   I know.
(*Beat*)
   Have a pastry. On me.

(*Stephen pulls out his money*)

STEPHEN: So that's 20 schillings.

MASHKAN: Nein. On me. Completely.

(*Stephen takes the pastry*)

STEPHEN (*serious*): Listen, Mashkan, I just want to say that these last few months—they've meant—

MASHKAN (*interrupting, said quickly*): Ja, ja, for me too. For me, too. . . . Sadness and joy.

STEPHEN: And music. Always music. No matter how inso-
lent I was or belligerent—

MASHKAN: Or pig-headed or self-absorbed—

STEPHEN: Okay, okay . . . still, I always learned something.

MASHKAN: I am getting a swelled head. Please go on.
(*Stephen and Mashkan laugh*)
Do you remember me comparing a musical composition
to a solid, well-constructed Viennese building?

STEPHEN: Of course.

MASHKAN: I told you both had flourishes and variations
which might appear to branch off aimlessly—but do not
be concerned; beauty lurks where you least expect to
find it. True in music—and in people, *Stephen** Hoff-
man.
(*Beat—this is a personal moment between these two men—
too personal. Mashkan breaks away from it*)
So, back to our final piece! Let us translate responsively.
I will start:
(*Said expansively—to mirror the feel of the music—which
is not heard*)
The old, wicked songs
The dreams, wicked and grim
Let us bury them!
Fetch me a large coffin

* Pronouncing it "Steven."

STEPHEN (*mischievously, to mirror feel of music*):
    I must put many things in it
    but I won't say what yet
    The coffin must be bigger
    than the great vat at Heidelberg!

(*As they get deeper into the poem, they become more animated, building off the other's enthusiasm*)

MASHKAN: And fetch me a bier
    made of tough, thick timber
    It must be even longer
    than the bridge at Mayence!

STEPHEN: And fetch me twelve giants
    They must be even stronger
    than St. Christopher in the Cathedral
    at Cologne on the Rhine!

MASHKAN (*holding his hands out as if holding the coffin*):
    They are to bear the coffin away
    and sink it into the deep sea!
    Such a large coffin
    needs a large grave

(*Mashkan continues to hold his hand out, in his own world*)

STEPHEN (*more personal, to mirror feel of music*):
    Do you know why this coffin
    should be so huge, so heavy?
    I am burying in it all my love . . .
(*Stephen truly sees Mashkan*)
    and all my pain.

(Mashkan continues holding his hands out; then finally releases the "coffin" and allows it to sink into the sea)

MASHKAN: Gut . . . Gut . . . And after these words—the piano solo.

(Mashkan takes the music and places it on the piano. Then he turns to Stephen)

You play.

(Stephen gingerly approaches the piano and sits down.

Stephen "caresses the piano now, instead of being rough with her."

Just as he's about to play he breathes and tugs three times.

Then Stephen plays)

MASHKAN *(as Stephen plays)*: It is your responsibility during this solo to release us from the sadness we have heard—make us remember the Poet's suffering, but give us a glimmer of hope that this experience will not completely destroy his life. Who knows, perhaps he will learn from it and move to a higher plane. Verstehst du, Stefan? Understand?

STEPHEN: Not completely.

MASHKAN: That is good. Question. Always question.
(As Stephen continues playing the "Andante espressivo" beautifully, Mashkan touches Stephen's head)
Definitely, a hat head.

(*Tongue-in-cheek*)
  And what a hat it will be.

(*Mashkan listens to Stephen's piano playing, lost in the music.*

The lights dim. There's a spotlight on Mashkan and on Stephen.

As the piece ends, they look at one another. The light goes out on Mashkan.

Then on Stephen

Then VIENNA)

The End

DATE DUE			

GAYLORD No. 2333   PRINTED IN U.S.A.